THE GREATEST PHILOSOPHER
WHO EVER LIVED

PETER J. KREEFT

The Greatest Philosopher
Who Ever Lived

IGNATIUS PRESS   SAN FRANCISCO

Cover art and design by Enrique J. Aguilar

© 2021 by Ignatius Press, San Francisco
All rights reserved
ISBN 978-1-62164-479-8 (PB)
ISBN 978-1-64229-182-7 (eBook)
Library of Congress Control Number 2021932255
Printed in the United States of America ∞

Contents

NINE SHORT
INTRODUCTIONS

THE POINT

I deliberately avoided putting her name on the front cover of this book in order to make you open the book to find out who she is. If you take two minutes to read to the next page, you will find out, and then you will have your reason either for slamming shut this book (and your mind) with disgust or for opening it (and your mind) with hope.

I recently wrote a four-volume history of philosophy for beginners covering the one hundred greatest philosophers who ever lived. I did not notice the most obvious thing that was common to every single one of them, however different they were in all other ways. Every one of them was a male.

I goofed.

Why? Not because justice is outraged at the exclusion of 50 percent of all the human beings who have ever lived. Perhaps the women were wise enough not to waste their time with philosophy because they had more pressing tasks, such as bringing these philosophers into existence in the first place, then nourishing them, educating them, and loving them into maturity and wisdom.

I goofed because I inexcusably forgot that "philosophy" is not the cultivation of cleverness or the sophistication of scholarship or the analysis of analysis or the refutation of refutations or the deconstruction of deconstructions. It is not a war of words marching out from the lip-gates of mental fortresses into endless battle against other words.

9

"Wisdom" is feminine (*sophia*). Philosophy is a romance, a love affair with Sophie.

Because I forgot this, I forgot her, the greatest philosopher who ever lived: Mary, the Mother of God and the Seat of Wisdom.

~

There have been tens of thousands of books about great philosophers and thousands of books about Mary, but as far as I know, not one in either class has classified Mary as a philosopher. This book is so unique among both of those two classes of books that you probably think it is simply a mistake, a misclassification, and a confusion, like classifying Karl Marx as a comedian or Groucho Marx as a revolutionary politician.

What is the first thing you think of when you think of philosophy on the human, subjective side? I'll bet it is not love. And what is the first thing you think of when you think of philosophy on the objective side, the side of the object loved? I'll bet it is not wisdom. I want to turn back your mind to Socrates or Aquinas (or almost anyone in between) when you think of philosophy, to the kind of thing that is no longer taught in most philosophy departments or written about in peer-reviewed philosophy journals or found among the philosophy books you find in bookstores. I want to make you think of the kind of thing Socrates lived and died for. If and only if I can do that, I think I can convince you that the greatest of all philosophers is Mary.

Here is my argument. It can be put in a single complex syllogism. Philosophy is the love of wisdom. Jesus is wisdom incarnate. Mary loved Jesus more than any other human being ever did. Therefore, Mary was the greatest philosopher (wisdom-lover) who ever lived. For she had the greatest love for the greatest wisdom.

Wisdom is not fleeting and fashionable but perennial and universal, for all ages and all people. Therefore, Mary's wisdom is as relevant to our age as to hers and as much to you as to professional philosophers. I will try to prove this in each of the fourteen basic divisions of philosophy that make up the fourteen basic chapters of this book by showing the connection between Mary's ancient wisdom and our modern problems, denials, and errors. No one's wisdom is more up to date than hers. No wonder the Devil fears her more than anyone else. Look what she did to his kingdom in ancient Canaan and in Aztec Mexico and in Nazi Germany. (I hope you were not so naïve as to think that those were merely natural, human evils!)

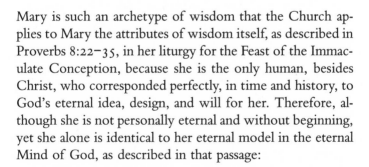

Mary is such an archetype of wisdom that the Church applies to Mary the attributes of wisdom itself, as described in Proverbs 8:22–35, in her liturgy for the Feast of the Immaculate Conception, because she is the only human, besides Christ, who corresponded perfectly, in time and history, to God's eternal idea, design, and will for her. Therefore, although she is not personally eternal and without beginning, yet she alone is identical to her eternal model in the eternal Mind of God, as described in that passage:

> The Lord possessed me in the beginning of his ways, before he made any thing from the beginning. I was set up from eternity, and of old before the earth was made. The depths were not as yet, and I was already conceived; neither had the foundations of waters as yet sprung out;

the mountains with their huge bulk had not as yet been established: before the hills I was brought forth: he had not yet made the earth, nor the rivers, nor the poles of the world. When he prepared the heavens, I was present: when with a certain law and compass he enclosed the depths: when he established the sky above, and poised the fountains of waters: when he compassed the sea with its bounds, and set a law to the waters that they should not pass their limits; when he balanced the foundations of the earth; I was with him forming all things: and was delighted every day, playing before him at all times, playing in the world: and my delights were to be with the children of men. Now therefore, ye children, hear me: Blessed are they that keep my ways. Hear instruction and be wise, and refuse it not. Blessed is the man that heareth me, and that watcheth daily at my gates, and waiteth at the posts of my doors. He that shall find me, shall find life, and shall have salvation from the Lord. (Douay-Rheims version)

Scripture describes many divine attributes. It is significant that of all the divine attributes it is wisdom that Mary personifies and it is wisdom that the Church selects to ascribe to Mary. (One of her titles is "Seat of Wisdom".) Wisdom is the specific goal of the philosopher.

Of course, Mary is much more than a philosopher. She is the Second Eve, the Mother of God, the Immaculate Conception, the Mediatrix of All Graces, and the Co-Redemptrix. But she is not less.

THE POINTER (ME)

But how dare I write a book about her? Is that not like a donkey writing a book about a dolphin? I would gladly read a book written by Beauty about the Beast, but this is a book written by the Beast about Beauty.

I thought of writing this book anonymously, but that seemed to me to be a kind of lie, by omission. I almost gave up the project. But then I remembered Saint Thomas Aquinas. After he saw God face to face in a mystical experience, he called his *Summa*, the greatest work of theology ever written, "straw". In his day, straw was used to cover up dung from horses, cows, or bulls. In other words, it covered bullshit. The S-word—*skubala* in Greek—is a "dirty word" because *skubala* is a dirty thing; but it is a perfectly *good* thing. God invented it, after all! The word is quite appropriate: it is used in the Bible: see Philippians 3:8 KJV. Any weaker word would weaken Paul's point. The thirteenth-century saint (Thomas) was making the same essential point as the first-century saint (Paul).

∼

In order to understand properly the holiest merely human being who ever existed, "our tainted nature's solitary boast" (in the worthy words of Wordsworth), one needs to be holy himself, and not a shallow, self-centered, silly, stubborn, stupid *schlemiel* like me. And to understand her mystical silence, one needs to be a silent mystic oneself, not a professional professor, a wordsmith, a gabbler, a chatterer, who has written an obscene number of books. Fake mystics usually gabble on and on, while true ones are content with silence, or at most a very few words. All the words of Jesus that we know He uttered could fit into half a page of a newspaper, and the only words He ever wrote were in the sand. He himself is called the "Word of God" (singular), not "the words of God" (plural). Words are important—they reveal and communicate our minds—but He did not save us by giving us His mind; He saved us by giving us His body. And where did He get His body? From Mary.

I write this book, not as an academic philosopher, but as a child who thinks he sees something profound and beautiful in Mary's largely silent wisdom and who wants to call out to others: "Oh, look!"—like a child seeing a rainbow or a cathedral for the first time.

Looking is better than talking. Lovers eventually tire of talking and retreat into the simplicity of silent, loving looking at each other. Of course, words are necessary and good for most of life, and, of course, conversation between friends is one of the best things in life; but there is something even better: Heaven is not called "the beatific conversation" but "the Beatific Vision".

When I look at Mary I see far less than is seen by the "seers"—the saints and mystics and prophets and poets—but I see *something*, and it is very beautiful. It is like a star.

∼

How, then, do we know the highest wisdom, if not primarily through words?

The greater the subject (e.g., faith, hope, charity, joy, peace, personhood, holiness, divinity, forgiveness, music, and humor as contrasted with math, money, entropy, engineering, ticks, politics, cars, and computers), the more one needs to understand it from within, not from without; by "connaturality", not by observation; by experience, not by science; by looking along it, not looking at it (to use the crucial distinction C. S. Lewis makes in his essay "Meditation in a Toolshed"); by "big picture" intuition, not by point-by-point abstract analysis; concretely, not abstractly— in other words, by a saint, not by a philosopher.

Why, then, do I dare to write this book? Why do I dare to rush in where angels fear to tread? There are three reasons. First, because I am indeed a fool, of course. But also, second, because I am a fascinated fool. The moth cannot help but be drawn to the flame. And finally, because God would not let me rest until I had done it.

"But Lord, you know that it is bound to be mainly only hot air."

"Indeed. But your readers are not angels. They are insects. Like you. They need a low-flying insect like yourself to speak their language. Many of them will read a second-rate writer like you even though they will not read My verbal angels, like Fulton Sheen and Frederick Faber and Bernard of Clairvaux and Louis-Marie de Montfort."

Never argue with God; you always lose.

When God commanded Balaam's ass to speak, what could the ass do but obey?

Introduction # 3

ABOUT PHILOSOPHY

Most books about Mary (there are thousands) are not written by philosophers. They say many things that are very true, good, and sometimes even beautiful, but not usually new or controversial or surprising. This one is different. (I say not "better", just "different".) Therefore, I need to justify it, to argue (we philosophers love to do that) for calling Mary a philosopher. That is not part of the picture we usually get about Mary. To "sell" my picture, I need to try to change your mind—not about Mary, but about philosophy.

I have to start by trying to turn your mind *backward* about philosophy because I believe that is the only way we can go *forward* and make progress. I am trying to create in your mind a mental time machine. Of course, literal time travel into the past is not only physically impossible but also logically impossible, because that could let you murder your own grandfather, and that would erase the existence of the murderer and, thus, of the murder. But perhaps time travel into the future is possible. Something like it happens, at least mentally, by suspended animation, as in the story of Rip Van Winkle. So let's imagine Socrates somehow Rip Van Winkled into the present. What would he think of our philosophy and our philosophers?

Philosophy today is a specialization, or a specialty—in fact it is so specialized that fewer than 4 percent of all American colleges and universities require anyone to take any philosophy at all. But for Socrates, "the love of wisdom" is not a "specialty". Socrates would be scandalized to learn that philosophy is now the business of "philosophy departments". Do we have a "love department"? Do we have an "air department"? A "life department"? Everyone needs wisdom even more than they need air or water or life itself. Does that sound ridiculous to you? Ask yourself this question: Is it not better to die as a wise man (or woman) than to live as a fool?

So this book is not for professional philosophers, i.e., for intellectual prostitutes like me, who sell their minds for money in classrooms and books. It is, like philosophy itself, for everyone. I have to keep reminding you that when I say "philosophy", I do not mean what goes on in most philosophy "departments"; I mean what goes on in the minds and lives of Socrates and his spiritual children. And that is why Mary is for everyone: because she is a true philosopher, and philosophy is for everyone.

Introduction #4

ABOUT FAITH AND REASON

Back in the eighteenth century, at the heart of the rationalism of the so-called "Enlightenment", the most brilliant and influential of modern philosophers, Kant, confessed that the Enlightenment's project of reason without faith, and of doing even "religion within the limits of reason alone", could not be carried out. He wrote that "human reason has this peculiar fate, that . . . it is burdened by questions which, as prescribed by the very nature of reason itself, it is not able to ignore, but which, as transcending all its powers, it is also not able to answer."

In other words, at the heart of purely rational philosophy there is a *koan* puzzle, a question that cannot in principle be answered.

Kant came to this conclusion because he denied that human reason could ever know objective reality, or "things-in-themselves". But even a more optimistic and robust (and commonsensical) notion of human reason, as able to know objective reality, must, if it is honest, quail and fail before at least two of the most personally demanding questions we can ask: *Who is God?* and *Does God love me?* Only religion rather than philosophy, and only faith rather than reason alone, can answer those questions.

Saint Augustine made the same *koan*-like point about the heart: that our heart, like Kant's reason, was restless until it attained what was impossible for it, until it rested in the

God who had made it for Himself; that, the human heart, by itself, was not capable of attaining the joy it most deeply desired.

Saints test reason by faith; philosophers test faith by reason. Saints ground reason in God, in divine revelation, known by faith. Philosophers ground faith by reason; they demand reasons for faith. And this is right, too, for we are commanded to be philosophers as well as saints in Scripture by the very first pope, Saint Peter: "Be ready always to give . . . a reason for the hope that is in you" (1 Pet 3:15, KJV). But if saints put faith first, while philosophers put reason first, how can Mary be a great philosopher?

Such a question is typically modern. Modern philosophers almost always see faith and reason as contrary if not contradictory, like two species of animals that cannot mate and often fight. They usually see religious faith as an obstacle to intellectual freedom, and dogmas as something like the laws tyrants impose rather than something like the intelligent, rational laws of nature, which science humbly and faithfully discovers by the mind rather than imposing by the will.

Saint John Paul II, in *Fides et Ratio*, a short summary of what all the great main-line Catholic philosophers in history have taught about the relationship between faith and reason, described these two human enterprises as being "like two wings on which the human spirit rises to the contemplation of truth". He then made the analogy with Mary, as the prime example of the essential theological principle that explains and justifies this wing-like cooperation, namely, the principle that God's supernatural grace and revelation always perfects rather than destroys, demeans, or ignores nature, especially human nature, and therefore also natural reason.

There is an analogy between Mary's self-description in response to the angel, "Behold the handmaid of the Lord" (Lk 1:38), and the classical medieval conception of natural reason and philosophy being the "handmaid" to supernatural revealed theology. A handmaid is not a slave but a free, willing servant, a helper, like Eve to Adam: a "helpmate" or "help meet [fit] for him" (Gen 2:18, KJV).

The relation between faith and reason, and between theology and philosophy, is analogous to the relationship between man and woman. But notice here how Mary transcends our stereotypes and expectations: we usually associate Mary, God's "handmaid", with faith rather than reason; but it is reason, and philosophy, that is the "handmaid" to faith and theology.

They are designed to be different but also to be married. They are like head and heart, like body and soul, and like individuality and sociality: each perfects the other when the relationship is right. Each rivals the other and fights with the other only when the relationship is wrong.

~

Philosophy is for everyone because everyone has a philosophy of life, a world view, and a life view. It may be wise or foolish, intelligent or stupid, true or false, good or bad. But if you say that "my philosophy is no philosophy", that is a philosophy, too: a foolish, stupid, and bad one.

And theology, and some kind of faith, is for everyone, too. If you say "I am an atheist; I have no faith", that is itself a faith. No one can begin with no assumptions at all. If you say you can, that is your assumption. Even Mary made one Assumption. (If you didn't get that in-house joke, ask a Catholic.)

Since philosophy is for everyone, and so is theology, Mary's example in relating these two enterprises is also for everyone. Mary is our perfect matchmaker.

ABOUT WISDOM

Religious philosophers and theologians, Jewish and Muslim as well as Christian, have traditionally distinguished three levels of wisdom.

The first is good philosophy, arrived at by our natural reasoning powers (all three "acts of the mind": understanding, judging, and reasoning).

The second is supernatural, divinely revealed theology, as distinct from natural theology, or natural reason reasoning about God without presupposing faith in any divine revelation. This second level of wisdom is explored by philosophical reason, but its data is based on divine revelation, a divine rather than a human initiative and starting point.

The third level is a supernatural gift of the Holy Spirit, "infused contemplation", in which wisdom (*sapientia* in Latin) is an actual "taste" (*sapere* in Latin) of the divine things we hope to attain and contemplate in Heaven. This is common in saints and mystics and ought to be common in ordinary Christians, too, for we are all called to this; but most do not know it or aspire to it.

Mary certainly had the third and highest kind of wisdom. Saint John Henry Newman, writing about Mary's title "Seat of Wisdom", said: "Mary has this title . . . because the Son of God, who is also called in Scripture the Word and Wisdom of God, once dwelt in her, and then, after His birth of her, was carried in her arms and seated in her lap in His first years. Thus, being, as it were, the human throne of Him who reigns in heaven, she is called the 'Seat of Wisdom'." (How delightfully literal!) This is why Saint John Paul II concluded *Fides et Ratio* with an invocation to Mary that she would be "a sure haven for all who devote their lives to the search for wisdom" on any of its three levels, including the first, the merely philosophical level.

To list all that the Bible says about wisdom we would need a very long book. A concordance of the KJV lists 223 references to wisdom (and about the same number of references to "wise"). And that does not even include the "second canon", or deuterocanonical books, the two longest of which are explicitly about wisdom and contain at least another 223.

The two most striking references are: (1) Job 28, a timeless classic about philosophy, i.e., the search for wisdom, and especially the contrast between our weakness in wisdom and our power in technology (yes, technology; even in that primitive, pre-technological age, the contrast was striking); and (2) 1 Corinthians 1, which *identifies* wisdom with Christ.

Introduction #6

THE DATA ABOUT MARY
IN SCRIPTURE

To list all the data in Scripture *about wisdom* would take a whole book, but to list all the data *about Mary* will take only a few pages.

This fact raises an obvious objection, especially from Protestants: How can Mary be so important if we have only 187 words from her, most of which are poetry?

The simplest answer is this: Because philosophy is the love of wisdom, and wisdom's natural home is silence.

As Lao Tzu said, "those who know, don't say; those who say, don't know." For "the Way that can be spoken is not the eternal Way" (*Tao Te Ching* 1). Job's greatest wisdom was expressed in these words: "I lay my hand on my mouth" (40:4), and "The words of Job are ended" (31:40). This wisdom (the wisdom of silence) is recognized by the verse "The Lᴏʀᴅ is in his holy temple; let all the earth keep silence before him" (Hab 2:20). We do not hear God when our own noise surrounds us—and the world is becoming increasingly noisy, and silence increasingly rare.

For Christians, wisdom is not, first of all, in words (which are plural and impersonal) but in the Word (Who is singular and a Person). And this Person is to be found in a most intimate way in Mary, both physically and spiritually, in her womb and in her will.

There are two kinds of silence: one negative, one positive.

The first is a lack, an emptiness; the second is an overplus, a fullness. The first is the silence of a rock or a beast; the other is the silence of a mystic. The first is beneath words; the second is beyond words.

Yet it is not opposed to words; in fact, it is the womb of words; it exists for words as a mother exists for a baby. God, who is beyond words, Himself expresses Himself perfectly in His Son, who is the Word of God. That is why I dare, like thousands before me, to put into the words of a book my wordy commentary on the nearly wordless wisdom of Mary, the greatest philosopher who ever lived. Mystic Mary was nearly wordless, but she was not Wordless.

~

The basis for all the rest of the Church's data is in her Scriptures. But they are only the most important part of her Sacred Tradition. For the same Church that authored and authorized the Scriptures and handed them down to us (that is what "tradition" literally means: "handed down") has also handed down to us the whole of the "Deposit of Faith" given by Christ through His authorized apostles and the successors *they* authorized, the bishops of the Church. That larger historical fact, which encompasses and justifies the Church's theology of Mary, is the simple and fundamental reason for a Christian to be a Catholic.

However, the data outside Scripture about Mary, namely the writings of the Church Fathers, the saints, the great theologians, and the official teaching of the Church in creeds and encyclicals, would require, not a book, not even a long one, but a library. So I shall be content here with the original, scriptural data. For the scriptural data are like tightly packed diamonds. Diamonds, like the texts about Mary, are rare but precious, and they are so hard and dense that (as Buddha put it in "The Diamond Sutra") they are the touchstone for all stones; they are the gems that can cut through all others while nothing else can cut through them.

By the way, in his "Diamond Sutra" Buddha radically missed identifying the "diamond" that cut through and shattered all other thoughts but which no other thought could cut through or shatter. For him, it was the doctrine (*dharma*) that "whatever is an arising thing, that is also a ceasing thing" —in other words, whatever has a beginning has an end. He was two-thirds right; for *samsara*, "birth and death", the universe of things and/or appearances, has both a beginning and an end; and Nirvana, or "the Buddha-mind", or "only-mind", has no beginning or end. But Buddha forgot *himself* and all other created persons, both human and angelic: they had a beginning (in being created) but will have no end. Buddha, the great and profound practical psychologist, failed to "know thyself."

The Words of Mary

The Christian scriptural data about Mary is twofold: the words *of* Mary and the words *about* Mary.

The words of Mary are few: only fifty-three in prose, in English translation, and 134 in poetry, in her Magnificat.

(1) Her question to the angel's Annunciation, "How can this be, since I have no husband?" (Lk 1:34).

(2) Her response to the angel's answer: "Behold, I am the handmaid of the Lord; let it be to me according to your word" (Lk 1:38).

(3) Her question to twelve-year-old Jesus in the Temple: "Son, why have you treated us so? Behold, your father and I have been looking for you anxiously" (Lk 2:48).

(4) Her prayer to Jesus at Cana: "They have no wine" (Jn 2:3).

(5) Her directions to the waiters at Cana: "Do whatever he tells you" (Jn 2:5).

(6) Her Magnificat (Lk 1:46–55):

> My soul magnifies the Lord,
> and my spirit rejoices in God my Savior,
> for he has regarded the low estate of his handmaiden.
> For behold, henceforth all generations will call me blessed;
> for he who is mighty has done great things for me,
> and holy is his name.
> And his mercy is on those who fear him
> from generation to generation.
> He has shown strength with his arm,
> he has scattered the proud in the imagination of their
>   hearts,
> he has put down the mighty from their thrones,
> and exalted those of low degree;
> he has filled the hungry with good things,
> and the rich he has sent empty away.
> He has helped his servant Israel,
> in remembrance of his mercy,
> as he spoke to our fathers,
> to Abraham and to his posterity for ever.

The Words about Mary

The words *about* Mary are bookended by two passages, one at the very beginning and one at the very end of history.

Mary stands, with Christ, in the middle. The passage in Genesis, at the beginning, is a prophetic prediction of this middle event. The passage in Revelation, at the end, is a retrospective look at it.

The first mention of Mary is in the first thing God said after the Fall of Adam and Eve. In Genesis 3:15, God said to the serpent (Satan) after the fall of the first Eve: "I will put enmity between you and the woman, and between your [spiritual] seed and her [biological as well as spiritual] seed; / he shall bruise your head, and you shall bruise his heel." (Yes, Achilles is a pagan foreshadowing of Christ.) The Fathers of the Church called Mary "the Second Eve" as Saint John Henry Newman, in his hymn "Praise to the Holiest in the Height", based on his poem "The Dream of Gerontius", called Christ the "second Adam". The name is based on Romans 5:12–21.

The other crucial Old Testament prophecy about Mary is Isaiah 7:14: "[T]he Lord himself will give you a sign. Behold, a virgin shall conceive and bear a son, and shall call his name Immanuel [God-with-us]."

The other "bookend", the last mention of Mary in the Bible, is Revelation 12:

> [1] And a great sign appeared in heaven, a woman clothed with the sun, with the moon under her feet, and on her head a crown of twelve stars; [2] she was with child and she cried out in her pangs of birth, in anguish for delivery. [3] And another sign appeared in heaven; behold, a great red dragon, with seven heads and ten horns, and seven diadems upon his heads. [4] His tail swept down a third of the stars of heaven, and cast them to the earth. And the dragon stood before the woman who was about to bear a child, that he might devour her child when she brought it forth; [5] she brought forth a male child, one who is to rule

all the nations with a rod of iron, but her child was caught up to God and to his throne, [6] and the woman fled into the wilderness, where she has a place prepared by God, in which to be nourished for one thousand two hundred and sixty days [3½ years]. . . . [13] And when the dragon saw that he had been thrown down to the earth, he pursued the woman who had borne the male child. [14] But the woman was given the two wings of the great eagle that she might fly from the serpent into the wilderness, to the place where she is to be nourished for a time, and times, and half a time [3½ years]. [15] The serpent poured water like a river out of his mouth after the woman, to sweep her away with the flood. [16] But the earth came to the help of the woman, and the earth opened its mouth and swallowed the river which the dragon had poured from his mouth. [17] Then the dragon was angry with the woman, and went off to make war on the rest of her offspring, on those who keep the commandments of God and bear testimony to Jesus.

Between these two "bookends" we find a few references to Mary in the Gospels:

Matthew 1:

[1] The book of the genealogy of Jesus Christ, the son of David, the son of Abraham. [2] Abraham was the father of Isaac . . . [16] and Jacob the father of Joseph the husband of Mary, of whom Jesus was born, who is called Christ. . . .

[18] Now the birth of Jesus Christ took place in this way. When his mother Mary had been betrothed to Joseph, before they came together she was found to be with child of the Holy Spirit; [19] and her husband Joseph, being a just man and unwilling to put her to shame, resolved to send her away quietly. [20] But as he considered this, behold, an angel of the Lord appeared to him in a dream,

saying: "Joseph, son of David, do not fear to take Mary your wife, for that which is conceived in her is of the Holy Spirit; [21] she will bear a son, and you shall call his name Jesus, for he will save his people from their sins." [22] All this took place to fulfil what the Lord had spoken by the prophet:

[23] "Behold, a virgin shall conceive and bear a son, / and his name shall be called Emmanuel"

(which means, God with us). [24] When Joseph woke from sleep, he did as the angel of the Lord commanded him; he took his wife, [25] but knew her not until she had borne a son; and he called his name Jesus.

Matthew 2:

[1] Now when Jesus was born in Bethlehem of Judea in the days of Herod the king, behold, Wise Men from the East came to Jerusalem. . . . [10] When they saw the star, they rejoiced exceedingly with great joy; [11] and going into the house they saw the child with Mary his mother, and they fell down and worshiped him. . . .

[13] Now when they had departed, behold, an angel of the Lord appeared to Joseph in a dream and said, "Rise, take the child and his mother; and flee to Egypt, and remain there till I tell you; for Herod is about to search for the child, to destroy him." [14] And he rose and took the child and his mother by night, and departed to Egypt, [15] and remained there until the death of Herod. This was to fulfil what the Lord had spoken by the prophet, "Out of Egypt have I called my son."

[16] Then Herod, when he saw that he had been tricked by the Wise Men, was in a furious rage, and he sent and killed all the male children in Bethlehem and in all that region who were two years old or under, according to the time which he had ascertained from the Wise Men. [17] Then was fulfilled what was spoken by the prophet Jeremiah:

[18] "A voice was heard in Ramah,
wailing and loud lamentation,
Rachel weeping for her children;
she refused to be consoled
because they were no more."

[19] But when Herod died, behold, an angel of the Lord appeared in a dream to Joseph in Egypt, saying, [20] "Rise, take the child and his mother, and go to the land of Israel, for those who sought the child's life are dead." [21] And he rose and took the child and his mother, and went to the land of Israel.

Luke 1:

[26] In the sixth month the angel Gabriel was sent from God to a city of Galilee named Nazareth, [27] to a virgin betrothed to a man whose name was Joseph, of the house of David; and the virgin's name was Mary. [28] And he came to her and said: "Hail, full of grace, the Lord is with you." [29] But she was greatly troubled at the saying, and considered in her mind what sort of greeting this might be. [30] And the angel said to her, "Do not be afraid, Mary, for you have found favor with God. [31] And behold, you will conceive in your womb and bear a son, and you shall call his name Jesus.

[32] He will be great, and will be called the Son of the
    Most High;
and the Lord God will give to him the throne of his
    father David,
[33] and he will reign over the house of Jacob for ever;
and of his kingdom there will be no end."

[34] And Mary said to the angel, "How can this be, since I have no husband?" [35] And the angel said to her,
"The Holy Spirit will come upon you,
and the power of the Most High will overshadow you;
therefore the child to be born will be called holy,
the Son of God.

[36] And behold, your kinswoman Elizabeth in her old age has also conceived a son; and this is the sixth month with her who was called barren. [37] For with God nothing will be impossible." [38] And Mary said, "Behold, I am the handmaid of the Lord; let it be to me according to your word." And the angel departed from her.

[39] In those days Mary arose and went with haste into the hill country, to a city of Judah, [40] and she entered the house of Zechariah and greeted Elizabeth. [41] And when Elizabeth heard the greeting of Mary, the child leaped in her womb; and Elizabeth was filled with the Holy Spirit [42] and she exclaimed with a loud cry, "Blessed are you among women, and blessed is the fruit of your womb! [43] And why is this granted me, that the mother of my Lord should come to me? [44] For behold, when the voice of your greeting came to my ears, the child in my womb leaped for joy. [45] And blessed is she who believed that there would be a fulfilment of what was spoken to her from the Lord." [46] And Mary said:

"My soul magnifies the Lord,
and my spirit rejoices in God my Savior,
for he has regarded the low estate of his handmaiden.
For behold, henceforth all generations will call me blessed;
for he who is mighty has done great things for me,
and holy is his name.
And his mercy is on those who fear him
from generation to generation.
He has shown strength with his arm,
he has scattered the proud in the imagination of their
    hearts,
he has put down the mighty from their thrones,
and exalted those of low degree;
he has filled the hungry with good things,
and the rich he has sent empty away.
He has helped his servant Israel,
in remembrance of his mercy,

as he spoke to our fathers,
to Abraham and to his posterity for ever."
[56]. And Mary remained with her about three months,
and returned to her home.

All of Luke 2 is narrative about Jesus, Mary, and Joseph:
the birth (1–7), the angels and shepherds (8–20), the cir-
cumcision (21), the presentation in the Temple (22–38), and
the finding of the twelve-year-old Jesus in the Temple (41–
52). The philosophically significant verse is 19: "Mary kept
all these things [the birth, with no room in the inn, and the
visit of the shepherds], pondering them in her heart." After
the finding in the Temple, it is again said that Mary "kept
all these things in her heart" (vs. 51). It is by far the longest
passage about Mary in Scripture—so long (52 verses) that
we do not print it out here. (A line must be drawn *some-
where*.) But be sure to reread it in your Bible. (If you don't
have one, steal one.)

John also adds the story of the wedding feast at Cana (Jn
2:1–11):

[1] On the third day there was a marriage at Cana in Galilee,
and the mother of Jesus was there; [2] Jesus also was invited to the marriage, with his disciples. [3] When the
wine failed, the mother of Jesus said to him, "They have
no wine." [4] And Jesus said to her, "O woman, what have
you to do with me? My hour has not yet come." [5] His
mother said to the servants, "Do whatever he tells you."
[6] Now six stone jars were standing there, for the Jewish
rites of purification, each holding twenty or thirty gallons.
[7] Jesus said to them, "Fill the jars with water." And they
filled them up to the brim. [8] He said to them, "Now
draw some out, and take it to the steward of the feast."
So they took it. [9] When the steward of the feast tasted
the water now become wine, and did not know where it

came from (though the servants who had drawn the water knew), the steward of the feast called the bridegroom [10] and said to him, "Every man serves the good wine first, and when men have drunk freely, then the poor wine; but you have kept the good wine until now." [11] This, the first of his signs, Jesus did at Cana in Galilee, and manifested his glory; and his disciples believed in him.

John also adds this detail from Jesus' crucifixion: "But standing by the cross of Jesus were his mother, and his mother's sister, Mary the wife of Clopas, and Mary Magdalene. When Jesus saw his mother, and the disciple whom he loved [John] standing near, he said to his mother, 'Woman, behold, your son!' Then he said to the disciple, 'Behold, your mother!' And from that hour the disciple took her to his own home" (19:25–27).

Mary is mentioned once more, in Acts 1:14, in the story of the descent of the Holy Spirit, her divine Spouse, at Pentecost: "All these [apostles] with one accord devoted themselves to prayer, together with the women and Mary the mother of Jesus, and with his brethren."

Everything else that we know about Mary begins with this data.

Introduction #7

A PERSONAL APPEAL

The most important preliminary requirement for understanding this book is that we turn back the clock (which Chesterton notes is eminently doable and desirable when the clock is keeping bad time) so that we think of philosophy as Socrates did, as the love of wisdom. This book will be quite unconvincing to you if you do not do that.

I must repeat this fundamental point, even though it may seem tiresome, because old bad mental habits are hard to break and cannot be erased simply by a single act of will, especially when they have become so comfortable that they seem more like skin than like clothing.

It is easy to parrot the formula ("philosophy" means "the love of wisdom") but hard to do the thing itself when most "philosophers" are doing another thing under the same name: logic games, linguistic analysis, scholarship, ideology, etc. It is surprisingly hard for us *not* to think of philosophy as the kind of thing we find today in philosophy textbooks, departments, classes, articles, doctoral dissertations, and professional journals. It is appallingly easy to forget the two most important things about philosophy: that it is a love and that it is about wisdom.

Socrates did not forget these two things. In the *Symposium*, he consents to speak about love only because he says it is the only thing he knows. How many philosophers today would or could say that? We usually seek *knowledge*, especially the knowledge about knowledge (epistemology, the focus of most modern philosophers); but even if we seek wisdom and not just knowledge, it is usually the wisdom about wisdom rather than the wisdom about love. We also sometimes love, but it is usually the love of love rather than the love of wisdom. (As Augustine says, "I was in love with love.") Instead of directing love to wisdom and wisdom to love, we direct wisdom to wisdom itself and love to love itself, thus giving to both of these noble things the disease of ingrown eyeballs.

So we must (1) restore love to our philosophy, and (2) restore philosophy (wisdom) to our love, not just to understand this book, but also to understand wisdom (which cannot be understood without love) and to understand love (which cannot be understood without wisdom).

A PREFACE FOR PROTESTANTS

Every Protestant I know "has issues" with Catholic devotion to Mary, even after it is explained to them that we Catholics do not *worship* her (*latria*), but we revere her more than any other merely human being (*hyperdulia*), because she is the Mother of God. For if, as all orthodox Christians believe, Jesus is literally a Divine Person as well as fully human, and if Mary is literally His mother, it logically follows that she is the Mother of God.

"God" means both (1) the single divine substance or essence or nature that is equally common to all three Divine Persons and (2) the personal name for the Father, the First Divine Person. "Jesus Christ is Lord" (*kyrios*, God) is meant in sense (1), not in sense (2).

No one was ever as close to God as Mary was, either physically or spiritually. She was almost unthinkably close to Him, as the Incarnation brought God almost unthinkably close to us. To deny her the title "Mother of God" is implicitly to deny Him His divinity.

But (the Protestant objects) in the whole New Testament, there are only a very few verses that speak of her. And she herself speaks hardly at all. There are far more words about Peter and about John the Baptist than there are words about Mary.

I do not believe in the Protestant principle of *sola scriptura* (that Scripture is our only infallible guide), which is the implied assumption of this argument; but I see the reasonableness of this scriptural objection for Protestants. It is so strong that almost every Protestant I know who became a Catholic, including myself, found Catholic devotion to Mary to be one of the last and hardest obstacles to overcome. And yet years later, nearly every one of those converts, including myself, looking back, cannot now understand why this devotion, which now seems so bright and beautiful, once loomed so large and threatening like a dragon. That is truly a puzzle, and neither Protestants nor Catholics seem to understand, at the same time in their lives, both the "before" and "after" stages of the radical change of attitude to Mary in the process of conversion. One of the secondary purposes of this book, if it works, is to solve that puzzle and answer that Protestant scriptural objection.

The answer, in brief, is that Mary's verbal economy in Scripture is providential and deliberate, not accidental; that it is part of her perfection; that the very fact that seems to Protestants to count against her, really counts for her: both for her own perfection and for her usefulness as our model in wisdom. Fake saints and mystics usually talk too much. Real ones are at home in humble, holy silence. They know that when they start arguing with God, His answer, though expressed more gently, is essentially the same as the words of a popular song: "Shut up and dance with Me!"

The deepest reason Protestants fear the Catholic exaltation of Mary in theory and the Catholic devotion to Mary in practice is that it seems to them to compromise the uniqueness of Christ. Scripture says that there is only one mediator between God and man, and that is Christ (1 Tim 2:5).

But Mary is not in the position of Christ, our mediator to God. She is in the position of ourselves, or a close and holy but wholly human friend, who can be our intercessor and thus "mediator" to Christ. "Mediator" does not necessarily mean "Redeemer". We mediate with each other in many ways. Mary can be our best, but not our only, human mediator to the one and only divine Mediator. If you deny that such human mediation is right, you deny the rightness of intercessory prayer.

Think of two partly interlocking circles. The one at the top is God; the one at the bottom is Man. Christ is the overlapping of the two circles. The lower circle, the human one, has five levels. The lowest is great sinners. Next comes little sinners. Then little saints. Then great saints. Finally, at the top, Mary. (*Somebody* has to be at the top; who has a better claim than she?) The only place the two circles overlap is Christ, not Mary.

There is absolutely nothing wrong with that theology. But there can be a wrong emphasis or attitude toward this Marian mediation. In the past, some Catholics, rightly believing in Christ's formidable divine justice but lacking an adequate personal intimacy and trust in His mercy, tried to mitigate their fear of Christ as just Judge by appealing to Mary's mercy instead. It is a serious theological as well as a pastoral error to contrast Mary's mercy with Christ's justice, as if she were indifferent to justice or as if He were unwilling to give mercy or as if she exceeded Him in mercy. But there are two profound truths at the root of this error.

One is the truth of intercessory prayer, which is based on the fact that each of us, especially the great saints and most especially Mary, can pray for us to God, and "the . . . prayer of a righteous man availeth much" (Jas 5:16 KJV). Mary's prayer to Christ at Cana, though only an implied request, was so powerful that she changed Christ's plans. When she presented to Him the embarrassing problem of running out of wine, He objected: "My hour [for public miracles] has not yet come." And yet He did her will and performed His first public miracle before He had planned to. She was the instrumental cause or catalyst for His first miracle. Of course, this change of His plans was part of His greater plan, His Providence; and His "objection" to her request was only a loving test of her trust. But by Christ's own will, His first miracle was an effect of Mary's human request as well as part of an earlier and larger divine plan. For God plans means as well as ends. The miracle would not have happened without her prayer. Christ is deliberately teaching us that here. The dependence of second causes (e.g., Mary) on the first cause (Christ) does not make the second causes unreal. In fact, it makes them real. "Prayer changes things" as much as any other human agency does. God has predestined our prayers to have real efficacy just as He predestines our works to have efficacy. (More accurately, He has destined rather than *pre*destined, since He is not in time.)

The other great truth in the piety of seeing Mary as the "mediator to the Mediator" is the justice and judgment of Christ. It is wrong to contrast mercy and justice either in Christ or in Mary or to minimize Christ's infinite mercy; but Christ's judgment is also clearly taught in Scripture (e.g., Jn 5:27, 30), and so is its fearsomeness (e.g., Rev 6:16). And we have largely forgotten that today. God does not ignore eternal justice. Justice is necessary. That is why the Cross is not an accident or a "tragedy" but a necessity.

"The fear of the Lord is the beginning of wisdom"— the principle is repeatedly stated in Scripture. This is not the fear of a slave but that of a son. It is awe and respect. When that rightful fear of the Lord as our Father is accompanied by a lack of trust, that is a fault, and a common one. And when that fault is made by the child, what is more natural for him than to seek his mother's intercession? And what is more natural for her than to give it? The analogy between family relations and religious relations is not accidental but God-designed.

~

The Catholic view of Mary is not heretical or idolatrous, as Protestants fear. Mary is not half human and half divine, Mary is wholly human. Mary is us.

Mary is also the Church, the communal Us. The Church is a "she", not an "it". She is "Holy *Mother* Church". Saint John Paul II was fond of saying that the Church's "Marian dimension" is "prior to her Petrine dimension". Mary is more important than all the Popes.

Christ is both perfect God and perfect Man; Mary is only perfect Man, or rather, perfect woman. Christ is not a woman, as Adam was not a woman. That is simply an undeniable historical fact. As He is the New Adam, Mary is the New Eve. That is her earliest title, in the words of the early Church Fathers.

Christ has two homes: his heavenly home and spiritual womb as eternally begotten of His divine Father and his earthly home and physical womb as temporally begotten of His human mother. He has no heavenly Mother. Although God has "feminine" as well as "masculine" attributes, since "the image of God" is not just male but "male and female" (Gen 1:27), yet God is not a Mother but a Father. That is divinely revealed. And it takes an egregiously inflated arrogance to correct God's own competence in naming Himself! And as Christ has no heavenly Mother, He has no earthly father. Joseph is not His biological father, only His foster father. Christ is the only begotten Son of His Heavenly Father alone, without a Mother, *and* the only begotten Son of His human mother alone, without an earthly biological father.

There are only four possibilities, logically: to be (1) both divine and human, (2) divine and not human, (3) human and not divine, or (4) neither human nor divine. Christ is the first. God the Father is the second, Mary, like us, is the third. Angels and rocks and numbers are the fourth.

Mary is not halfway between us humans and Christ, something standing between divine and human beings, like an angel (which is how some mistakenly "spiritual" people think of Christ). Nor is she half divine and half human, like a Greek mythological hero (which is how some other mistaken people think of Christ). Nor is she wholly divine and wholly human (which is the correct way to think of Christ). Mary is not Christ or half Christ; she is human and wholly human, but perfectly human.

The first cause of her perfection, of course, was not herself but God. But divine grace does amazing and fantastic things. Never, never put limits on it! That is my fundamental answer to Protestants' objections to the Church's high view of Mary, whom God's angel addressed as "*full* of grace". She is like the water jars at Cana, filled "up to the brim", to the limit of the human.

There is much more to say about Mary and Protestantism, but I will say only one more thing in this book. It is the surprising claim that Mary, far from separating the different churches and denominations, will be the primary cause of their reconciliation. She is alive and active and powerful and longs for her beloved children to come together and heal their divisions.

When I made this point one time to an audience that was

mainly Protestant, I could hear everyone stop breathing for a moment. My previous explanations of Catholic Marian theology had been received with polite and open-minded nods. This point, I could see, was a shock. It brought her too close for comfort, made her too real.

Warren Carroll's *Our Lady of Guadalupe and the Conquest of Darkness* tells the incredibly dramatic story of what Mary did five centuries ago in Aztec Mexico. (It will make a great movie someday.) She is "the patroness of the Americas", and the Americas need her very badly again, now that the same evil spirit that inspired the Canaanites and the Aztecs with their human sacrifice are rising again.

Our children were never more in need of their heavenly Mother. We kill one-third of them, in the womb—the same percentage of children that the Aztecs killed. The womb used to be the supreme place of safety and comfort. Now it is the most dangerous death camp on earth. How can anyone think that this Mother neglects her children? If she is the closest saint to God in Heaven, as she was on earth, then she has the greatest share in all three of God's attributes of wisdom, love, and power. How could she be ignorant of her children? How could she be loveless or indifferent to their fate? How could she be powerless when she is as close to God as any creature can be?

Protestants are soldiers of the same Christ that we Catholics worship and obey, and they are called to follow the same Joan of Arc into battle. You do not need to solve the problems of Marian theology or of Catholic ecclesiology to enlist in her army, especially in an emergency like this, which is literally a matter of life or death. Join us. We have a common enemy. We need you to fight with us.

THE FOURTEEN GREAT
QUESTIONS OF PHILOSOPHY

A complete philosophy manifests wisdom in answering the basic questions in each of the major areas of philosophy, i.e., (1) methodology, (2) epistemology, (3) logic, (4) metaphysics, (5) philosophical theology, (6) cosmology, (7) philosophical anthropology, (8) philosophical psychology, (9) ethics, (10) political philosophy, (11) philosophy of history, (12) philosophy of education, (13) aesthetics, and (14) philosophy of religion.

The short version of the central question in each field is as follows.

1. Methodology (practical epistemology): What means or methods attain our goal of wisdom?
2. Epistemology: What is knowing?
3. Logic: How should we order our thoughts in relation to each other?
4. Metaphysics: What is Being? What is the nature of reality? What truths about reality are universal?
5. Philosophical theology: What can our natural reason know about God?
6. Cosmology: What are the most fundamental principles of the material universe in which we live?
7. Philosophical anthropology: What is man? (and woman?)

8. Philosophical psychology: What is the soul or psyche? How should we use it?
9. Ethics: What is the good for man? And how should we live and behave in order to attain it?
10. Political philosophy: What is a good state? How should we live in a bad one?
11. Philosophy of history: What are the causal forces by which human history works?
12. Philosophy of education: How do we best educate our children?
13. Aesthetics: What is beauty, both natural and artificial?
14. Philosophy of religion: What is the essence of religion, i.e., our relationship with God?

Mary gives us the very best possible answer to all fourteen of these questions. The longer version of these questions is as follows.

1. *Methodology* is practical, not theoretical. "The end justifies the means" here. The cliché that "the end does not justify the means" means only that in ethics a good end does not justify an intrinsically evil means. But the end in general justifies the means in general; that is what a "means" *means*! So if the end is wisdom, what is the best means to it? That is the right question for a philosopher to ask.

2. *Epistemology*, the study of knowledge, the science of knowledge, or the knowledge of knowledge, is mainly theoretical (what *is* knowledge?); but it also has a practical dimension, which is essentially methodology (point [1]). Mary has nothing to say explicitly about theoretical epistemology, which is, to most people, the most abstract and dull of all the divisions of philosophy. (And so it is, of course, the division in which most contemporary philosophers specialize!)

3. *Logic* is not only about the rules of reasoning but also about the formal structure of thinking. What does wise thinking look like? This is a much more concrete and practical ("existential", human) question than the supremely abstract laws of thought like the law of noncontradiction and the law of identity. This practical question is about the forms, or the order, that wise thought takes. And since it is about the form of thought rather than the content, it is properly classified as part of logic. Logic is about the relation of thoughts to each other; the rest of philosophy is about the relation of thought to reality. Logic has existential consequences. For as Buddha said in the *Dhammapada*, "All that we are depends on our thoughts." No one's thoughts were ever better ordered than Mary's. She is not irrelevant to logic.

4. *Metaphysics* is about the nature of reality as such, or being qua being, i.e., all being, being universally rather than different beings and kinds of beings. This sounds supremely abstract. But some metaphysics is always presupposed or implied in the rest of philosophy. (So is some epistemology, by the way.) Some controversial questions of metaphysics are: the reality or unreality of matter, spirit, manyness, oneness, nature, supernature, and causality.

5. *Philosophical theology.* Since metaphysics is about being, it culminates in the study of the nature and existence or nonexistence of an ultimate being—in other words, God or something like God—that functions as the absolute, the standard or touchstone for all being. This is philosophical theology.

The central question of metaphysics is the nature of reality as such: What makes anything real? If the answer is something like God, then metaphysics leads to philosophical theology. "What is God?" was the question Thomas

Aquinas asked his monastic teachers at the age of four, and, not satisfied with their answers, in order to find better ones, he became Saint Thomas Aquinas.

No one, not even Aquinas, can show us who God is better than Mary can because no one was closer to God than she, not only spiritually but even physically. She was His mother! Mary's answer to the question "What is God?" is not a set of words that she spoke; it is her baby. "In him all the fulness of God was pleased to dwell" (Col 1:19). When Catholics long to see God, they ask Mary to "Show us the blessed fruit of thy womb, Jesus." That is her ultimate purpose.

6. *Cosmology*, like metaphysics, is practical as well as theoretical: it is not only about the nature of the universe, but also about how it affects our lives. It is about our fundamental attitude toward "all that is here below", the concrete whole that is the cosmos, of which physics is only an abstract aspect. Cosmology has a practical as well as a theoretical dimension. Practical cosmology is to theoretical cosmology as sailing or surfing is to oceanography: it is about how to surf or sail on the waves of the ocean of time, which are the waves of God's Providence. Mary surfed on the waves of Divine Providence better than anyone else. Surfers learn from other surfers more than from books.

7. *Philosophical anthropology* (as distinct from scientific, historical anthropology) is about the nature, value, and destiny of man. These are "practical" or "existential" questions. How ironic to confine anthropology, the science of the human subject, to questions that are not about man the subject but only man the object! It is not unreasonable to demand an impersonal view of impersonal things like numbers, machines, or planets, but it seems unreasonable to demand only an impersonal view of the person. If Mary was

"our tainted nature's solitary boast", we can learn more from her than from anyone else about who we are, except from her Son, who reveals perfectly not only who God is but also who we are. He is the perfect man and she is the perfect woman.

8. *Philosophical psychology* (as distinguished from scientific psychology or empirical psychology) can be included under philosophical anthropology, since both are about man; but it can also be distinguished from it by its focus on the psyche or soul and its relation to the body. It can also be classified as the practical dimension of anthropology, as methodology can be classified as the practical dimension of logic and religion the practical dimension of theology.

9. *Ethics* is, of course, about (a) good and evil or (b) right and wrong or (c) ought and ought not. And which of these three pairs of opposites one chooses to begin with determines the kind of ethical system one will have, whether the central concepts will be (a) the goods of virtue and happiness (flourishing, *eudaimonia*), as in Aristotle, or (b) rights, laws, and freedoms, as in Locke, or (c) duty and obligation, as in Kant. Obviously, all three are legitimate and important.

Nietzsche is right to say that to understand anyone's philosophy, even his metaphysics, one should ask what ethics it leads to. Wisdom, the goal of philosophy, is precisely this joining of theory and practice, metaphysics and ethics. And we all know that we do in fact learn this wisdom more by concrete human examples than by abstract impersonal principles. And Mary is our very best merely human example for ethics.

10. *Political philosophy* is about the state and how the individual and the family are and ought to be related to it. It is not about social utility or efficiency or "realpolitik", but is the civic or public aspect of social *ethics*. Like ethics in

general, it is both theoretical and practical. Its theoretical part may sound Utopian (about "the ideal state"), but its practical part includes guidance in our relating to non-Utopian regimes like the Roman tyranny under which Mary lived.

11. *Philosophy of history* is, rather unsurprisingly, about history; and its ultimate question is the whence and the whither, the alpha and omega, the beginnings and the end of history, including the source of its causality. Is anyone in charge of it? Is history "His story", or is it just "one damned thing after another"? In either case, how do I fit into it if Christ is the key to history, as Augustine argued in the classic Christian philosophy of history, *The City of God*, and as Chesterton argued in his masterpiece *The Everlasting Man*? If Mary was the primary "fit" of humanity into Christ, both biologically and spiritually, and Christ is the key to history, then Mary is also the key to the philosophy of history.

12. *Philosophy of education* is about the who, what, where, when, and why of teaching and educating our children. Its practical part deals, not with ideal systems, but with existing educational structures and methods, both public and private, formal and informal. First among these, until modern times, has always been the family.

13. *Aesthetics* is the division of philosophy that studies beauty, both natural and artificial (the arts). But while the theoretical question is: What is beauty? the practical question is: How do we and our lives become beautiful? If the most beautiful thing we can know is the soul and the life of a saint, and if Mary is the greatest saint, then she is the touchstone for beauty.

14. *Philosophy of religion* is about "religion", which means literally "a binding relationship", our personal relationship with our God, both individual and collective and both in-

visible (inner) and visible (outer, institutional), and about the relation between these two dimensions.

These are not philosophy's only questions, but they are fourteen of the most important, controversial, and pressing. Of these three adjectives, "important" is the most important (!), for it means "life-changing". As William James so commonsensically says, if it makes no difference to your life whether you believe an idea to be true or false, then that idea is for all practical purposes neither true nor false to you. The essential *nature* of truth in general (a major question in theoretical epistemology) is clearly the match between the subjective idea and the objective reality (this is called epistemological realism or common sense realism); but the "size" of any particular truth, so to speak, is the size of the difference it makes in our practice, our lives.

And in each case, Mary shows us the best answer: in her words, in her silence, in her deeds in her earthly lifetime, and in her deeds after her lifetime.

All this is not just a philosophical game. Mary will change your life.

MARY'S PHILOSOPHY

Chapter I

MARY'S METHODOLOGY

This chapter is the longest one in the book, and it has the most sections. Why? Because it is the most practical. "Practical" means that it works, as a means to attain the end, which for philosophy is wisdom.

How did Mary become so wise? What means, what method, what spiritual technology, did she use?

Some philosophers have distinct methods for doing philosophy. The Sophists' method is sneaky fallacies and tricks. Socrates' method is step-by-step logical questioning, beginning with definitions of terms. The medieval Scholastic method is summarized in the structure of a *Summa* article, which is essentially an abbreviated, summarized Socratic debate. The Baconian method is to expand our empirical data base by experimentation and to use inductive reasoning. The Cartesian method is to begin with universal doubt, find a self-evident principle, and deduce everything from that, imitating mathematics as much as possible, using only clear and distinct ideas. The Kantian method is to seek the fundamental conditions of possibility for experience on the side of the subject of consciousness. The phenomenological method (the early Husserl) is to find the irreducible essences or natures behind ordinary experienced phenomena. The pragmatic method is to judge ideas by their consequences in life. The ideal language method (Russell and the early Wittgenstein) is to translate everything into an ideally clear logical language. G. E. Moore's alternative method of linguistic analysis is the slow, careful, demanding, exact analysis of ordinary language and common sense. The method of deconstructionism is "the hermeneutic of suspicion" that asks of every idea that claims objective and impersonal truth how it serves the power interests of race, class, or gender.

All these methods, however different, have one thing in common: they are a kind of intellectual technology; they treat philosophy as an impersonal science more than as a personal love of wisdom. Mary's method is different. The one it most closely resembles is the Socratic method. The rabbinic method with which she was familiar resembled it in many ways.

There are at least fourteen implicit principles to Mary's method for learning wisdom. They are:

1. Tradition
2. "The fear of the Lord"
3. Contemplative receptivity
4. Active questioning
5. Silence
6. "Pondering"
7. The inner life
8. Openness to grace
9. Closeness to Christ
10. Virginity
11. Innocence
12. Faith
13. Obedience
14. Accepting suffering

1. Tradition

This is where all wisdom does in fact begin for every one of us. None of us is Adam. We are born into a world, a culture, and a family, which "hand down" or "hand over" their wisdom to us, like the baton in a relay race. Mary inherited the wisest tradition, the one authored and authorized by God, a divine "revelation" or self-disclosure. Its primary medium was divinely inspired Scriptures, which Mary knew and loved. According to these Scriptures, it was nothing less than divine and eternal wisdom (which was about to be incarnated in Christ) that had empowered all the great prophets, saints, and sages of Israel, many of whom (especially Moses and Elijah) were instruments by which God worked public miracles.

Chapter 11 of the "Wisdom of Solomon" is typical of these Scriptures. It summarizes the long history of wisdom in Israel's great spiritual ancestors: Adam, Abel, Noah, Abraham, Lot, Jacob, Joseph, Moses, David, Solomon. It is the whole Old Testament in miniature.

Even though this wisdom was divine and eternal, it also reached down into time and history. This had happened only in Judaism and not in paganism. Even the Greek *Logos*, or eternal truth, remained deistically removed and abstract, an ideal rather than an active force in history. But in Israel, wisdom was historical. The Jewish saints and sages were previews of the destined Incarnation of Divine Wisdom, Who through Mary is revealed to be, not just an abstract, eternal divine attribute, but a concrete, historical Divine Person with a human nature.

This shatters our typically Greek expectations and categories, which separate the eternal from the temporal and historical. In the Jewish Scriptures, Wisdom is not just a timeless, eternal abstraction, nor is it just a concrete

historical, temporal person like Solomon. It is ultimately revealed as bridging that gap. That is the Incarnation, and it
happened in Mary. Mary became the mother of Wisdom
Himself.

The Incarnation was not an anomaly, for already in Old
Testament Judaism, Wisdom was both divinely eternal and
also historically temporal. For instance, in "The Wisdom
of Sirach" (chap. 24), Wisdom's eternity and Wisdom's
historicity are the twin themes: "Wisdom . . . is honored
in God and will glory in the midst of her people. . . . I
[Wisdom] came forth from the mouth of the Most High
. . . before all creatures . . . an unfailing light . . . in high
places. . . . The Creator of all things . . . assigned a place for
my tent. And he said, 'Make your dwelling in Jacob, and in
Israel receive your inheritance, and among my chosen put
down your roots.'"

This Divine Wisdom became incarnate, not just in the
world in general or in "humanity" in general, but *in Mary*.
She is the "Seat of Wisdom" as no saint or sage or prophet
ever was or can be because she was the seat of Christ, Who is
Wisdom itself—not just wise, not just wiser than Solomon,
not just the wisest man who ever lived, but Wisdom Itself.
(Saint Paul refers to "Christ Jesus whom God made our
wisdom": 1 Cor 1:30). Wisdom is a Person! Christ does
not merely *teach* us wisdom, He *is* our Wisdom. And He,
the Divine Wisdom, the ultimate object of all philosophy
that is true to its honorable name ("the love of wisdom"),
can be in us only because He is first in her.

And that was not just a one-time past and dead and accidental event. It continues. As Christ continues to operate
in His Church, He does not leave His Mother behind, like
a taxi or a horse.

For not only did Mary, the Seat of Wisdom, give us Wisdom Itself, her Son, but her Son then gave us His seat, Mary, from *His* seat, His throne, on the Cross. "When Jesus saw his mother, and the disciple whom he loved [John] standing near, he said to his mother, 'Woman, behold, your son!' Then he said to the disciple, 'Behold, your mother!' And from that hour the disciple took her to his own home" (Jn 19:26–27). From the beginning of the Church, Christians, since they called themselves *His* brothers, called Mary *their* mother.

That, too, was not a one-time event, a past, dead, historical accident. It continues. Just as the Church's "handing down" of her Tradition is the handing-down, not just of words about Christ, but of Christ Himself, especially in Baptism and the Eucharist, so the same is true of Mary, and of "Behold, your Mother."

2. *"The Fear of the Lord"*

It is repeated many times in the Jewish Scriptures: "The fear of the Lord is the beginning of wisdom." Philosophers like Aquinas define fear as the opposite of love. Fear is repulsion, or the "irascible" appetite, whether irrational and involuntary or rational and voluntary, as love is attraction, the "concupiscible" appetite, whether irrational and involuntary (which we share with the animals) or rational and voluntary (which we do not). The philosophers also distinguish two kinds of fear: servile fear, which is the slave's fear of receiving pain or harm from his master, and filial fear, which is the fear of offending or disappointing a beloved father, human or divine. Thus the lower form of "the fear of the Lord" (servile fear) is to be replaced by the higher form (filial fear), since "perfect love casts out fear" (1 Jn

4:18). But unless it is first there, it cannot be cast out. We begin at the bottom, not at the top.

There is also a third kind of fear, which is more primordial. It is awe. All premodern peoples felt it, but today we feel it less and less, and it is becoming simply incomprehensible for secularists, who praise us for "coming of age", progressing, and growing out of it. But it would be better to pity us for regressing and *shrinking* out of it. It is no accident that we call our psychiatrists "shrinks".

This primordial fear is what Rudolf Otto, in *The Idea of the Holy*, calls "the numinous". It is the awe and wonder that moves us to bow or kneel or hide our faces before the presence of something greatly superior and mysterious. We feel this fear even before we distinguish between its filial form and its servile form. To understand this primordial fear, think of the distinction between the fear of a ghost and the fear of a crocodile. No ghost can physically harm us, as a crocodile can, yet we fear it. Why? It is not the fear of what it may do to us, but the fear of it simply being what it is. When angels appear in Scripture, if they are not mistaken for men they elicit this fear, and their first words to us usually have to be "Fear not!"

As Chesterton says,

> The Fear of the Lord, that is the beginning of wisdom, and therefore belongs to the beginnings, and is felt in the first cold hours before the dawn of civilisation; the power that comes out of the wilderness and rides on the whirlwind and breaks the gods of stone; the power before which the eastern nations are prostrate like a pavement; the power before which the primitive prophets run naked and shouting, at once proclaiming and escaping from their god; the fear that is rightly rooted in the beginnings of every religion, true or false: the fear of the Lord, that is the begin-

ning of wisdom; but not the end. (*Saint Thomas Aquinas: The Dumb Ox*)

But no one can end at the end without beginning at the beginning.

This primordial fear or awe is neither the merely irascible (repellent) or the merely concupiscible (attractive), for in it we feel both an attraction and a repulsion at once, like being caught between incoming and outgoing tides. Its attraction is not like that of a comforting teddy bear or a warm bath, and its repulsion is not like that of disgust or hate. It is the emotional stimulus toward worship and adoration. It is the first psychological origin of religion. And it is dying in our culture and in our souls, and so is religion, its fruit.

It is dying in our culture *because* it is dying in our souls, since culture is made by us, who have souls. It is also dying in our souls because it is dying in our culture, since culture shapes and educates souls.

But it was not dying or dead in Mary. She was very familiar, both in her Scriptures and in her experience, with the truth that "the fear of the Lord is the beginning of wisdom."

3. Contemplative Receptivity

A third method or way to wisdom is the most fundamental of all. It is metaphysical, or ontological; that is, it is an attitude toward being, toward being as such, toward all being. We might regard it as the abstract and universal version of the fear of the Lord. It is the fear, or respect, that is directed to whatever is real. We could call it "contemplative receptivity" if we wanted to sound scholarly. It is not a demanding and active attitude that wants to change the nature of reality but the humble, receptive attitude that lets it teach us. Its justification is simply that for Mary "reality" meant God first of all, because God created and designed it all. Thus her attitude toward God was the model for her attitude toward His creation: to respect it and humbly learn from it—which means to conform to its principles rather than to judge it, criticize it, complain of it, demand things of it, manipulate it, or reinvent it.

Francis Bacon and other founders of the modern mind turned this wisdom backward (though the history books call them "forward-looking"!) and criticized this contemplative and "conforming" task as childish, immature, passive, and weak. For him, the purpose of knowledge was not truth but power, and man's primary task on earth was not wisdom but "the conquest of Nature" through science and technology. He probably would have called Frodo and his companions childish for refusing the Ring of Power and would have admired Sauron for inventing it.

Goethe followed this "activist" heresy by changing the first verse of John's Gospel from "In the beginning was the Word" to "In the beginning was the Deed."

C. S. Lewis, in his prophetic book *The Abolition of Man*, saw this radical turnaround, which amounted to nothing less than a new and different answer to the single most important question in human life, the question of the *summum bonum*, or greatest good, in these words "For the wise men of old the cardinal problem had been how to conform the soul to reality, and the solution had been knowledge, self-discipline, and virtue. For magic and applied science alike the problem is how to subdue reality to the wishes of man: the solution is a technique" (i.e., technology). The critical point will be reached when our conquest of nature includes a conquest of our own human nature. Transgenderism is only the beginning. Already our most "progressive" thinkers are seriously speaking of "transhumanism" and artificial immortality.

This is the crucial message of the greatest book of the twentieth century, *The Lord of the Rings*. We are drawn to that book as to a mirror, for we are Sauron, and we have forged our own Ring of Power, and that is our addiction and our fate. We have changed the grammar of being; it is now no longer in the nominative case but in the possessive case. Our primary word toward being is not Mary's *fiat* ("let it be!")—or, in relation to God, "Yours!"—but that of the seagulls in *Finding Nemo*. It is the word "mine!" We are saying to God, "You are in *my* seat."

This is the cosmic, or universal, reversal of our fundamental attitude toward being as such. It is the exact opposite of Mary's *fiat*, which was her response, not only to the special vocation given to her through God's angel, but also to all reality. For she knew that all reality was God's reality, since He was its Creator; that all truth was God's truth, since He was its designer; and that He was the agent of an all-encompassing, omniscient, and benign Divine Providence, to which she totally, trustingly abandoned herself. (De Caussade's title is not too strong: "*Abandonment* to Divine Providence".) She "knew" this wisdom not only by reason, in her mind, as an abstract principle, but personally and concretely, by experience, in her heart, and by her love (love is not blind; love *sees*) and by the free consent of her will that yields both the deepest wisdom and the deepest joy.

4. Active Questioning

There are two very different assumptions behind asking questions, whether the question is addressed to a person or to an idea. When two persons are involved, the question is asked either in the spirit of a student or in the spirit of a prosecuting attorney. The student questions the teacher under the assumption that the teacher speaks the truth, while the prosecuting attorney questions a hostile witness under the assumption that he does not.

There are also two ways of questioning *ideas*. We can assume the idea is true until we prove it false, as Socrates does, or we can use Descartes' "universal methodic doubt", which is a principle of the scientific method, and treat all ideas as false until we prove them true.

Some people confuse these two situations by treating people with the suspicion that is due to ideas in the scientific method, but many more people treat ideas with the "non-judgmental" faith that is fitting for trustable people. This is why so few people today understand the principle "love the sinner but not the sin" and "hate the heresy but not the heretic." The Inquisition treated heretics as if they were heresies, without rights (for "error has no rights", but people in error do). Today we make the same mistake in the opposite direction: we treat heresies as if they were heretics, with rights. We apply "judge not" to ideas instead of people —especially when these ideas are principles of sexual immorality. (I first wrote "sexual morality", but then realized that for contemporary culture, that is an oxymoron.)

Religious faith treats ideas from God as true and questions them, not to refute them, but to explore them, to come to understand them better. At the opposite pole, the scientist, like the attorney, questions ideas in order to test them as severely as possible and prove them false if possible. In between is the neutral position that is the method we usually use in conversation with our fellow human beings who are neither God nor criminals on trial.

Unbelievers accuse believers of naïveté and a lack of questioning, but unbelievers need as much faith to assume that God is not real as believers need to assume that He is. Believ-

ers arrive at their position through questioning just as unbelievers do, and often question their theistic faith more, not
less, than unbelievers question their atheistic faith, because
unbelievers are under the illusion that they have no faith
to question, that unbelief is the self-evidently right starting
point. *That* is naïve. It is also arrogant.

The controversial methodological question for philosophy
is which of the two methods, the Socratic or the Cartesian,
the conversational or the scientific, should be used. Are ideas
to be believed until shown to be false or disbelieved until
shown to be true? The controversial question for religion is
the relationship between its method (faith) and reason, especially reason's Socratic curiosity. (Obviously, the Cartesian method, which is appropriate in the laboratory and in
the courtroom, is not appropriate for divine revelation, for
God is neither in the dock nor in a test tube.) Some people (usually unbelievers) say that faith fears questions; others (usually strong believers) say that it welcomes them and
revels in them.

The rabbis have always taken the latter line, anticipat-
ing the Socratic method with their method of teaching by
questioning. Mary's questioning proceeds from that kind of
strong faith. It is rabbinic.

There are very few references in Scripture to Mary speaking, and in three of them, she asks questions. She asks a question to the angel of the Annunciation, to her twelve-year-old
Son in the Temple, and implicitly to Him at the wedding feast
at Cana. (The question implied in "They have no wine" is:
What are you going to do about that?)

All three have a hidden assumption, and all three times
the assumption is faith: in the angel, in Jesus at twelve, and
in Jesus at thirty.

There is also, of course, curiosity and truth-seeking as

well as faith in the complex set of motives behind her questioning. There is the juxtaposition of her humble knowledge of her own ignorance with her strong desire to escape it. This is honest, humble, and praiseworthy curiosity, as distinct from the "vain curiosity" that the ancients labeled a fault because it is motivated by pride and the arrogant demand to know it all, whether or not that knowledge is good for us and fit for us.

In terms of method, the very best way to get an answer that is true is to ask God, especially when He is incarnate! The next best way is to ask an angel. After that, in descending order, ask a prophet, a saint, a teacher, a priest or rabbi, or a good friend.

When Mary asked the angel of the Annunciation how this would happen without her breaking her vow of virginity, she was not doubting or disrespecting God or His angel. She was in the same state of mind and heart as Socrates when he heard, from his friend, the almost equally surprising verdict of the Delphic oracle that there was no one in the world wiser than he. Both Socrates and Mary wanted to reconcile their faith in divine revelation with their own reason and experience, which seemed to contradict it. They would not simply deny or ignore either one of these two sources of truth. Socrates knew by experience that he had no wisdom, yet he could not simply deny his faith in the divinely inspired oracle's authority. Mary knew by experience in hearing the angel that she would become pregnant, but she could not simply violate her religious vow of virginity.

As we shall see in the next chapter, both Socrates and Mary exemplified the logic of paradox and its transforming of a simple, obvious either/or into a mysterious both/and. Both Socrates and Mary had to reconcile two pieces of apparently (but not really) contradictory data. Socrates had data from his self-knowledge and also from the oracle. Mary had data from her vow and also from the angel. Neither took the easy way out by denying any part of the data. That is why they actively questioned, not the truth, but the meaning, of the divine revelation. This is the questioning that is utterly compatible with piety and sanctity, not at all counter to it or a temptation against it.

We must integrate all the truths we know and believe, or else we become disintegrated in mind. We must integrate all our goods and moral duties, or else we become disintegrated in our will. We must integrate all our loves under one supreme love, or else we become disintegrated in our heart. Both Socrates and Mary demanded and attained this integration by their questioning.

Even the politically naïve but philosophically profound agnostic Martin Heidegger perceived that thinking, especially passionately questioning thinking, is a vocation, a calling, which presupposes some sort of caller—if not a personal God, then (for him) a kind of impersonal Fate. He wrote: "The question 'What calls on us to think?' strikes us directly, like a lightning bolt" (*What Is Called Thinking?*)

5. Silence

There is no wisdom without listening, and there is no listening without silence (you can not listen and speak at the same time), and therefore there is no wisdom without silence.

Silence is not just the absence of speech. Silence is a whole world. Max Picard wrote a profound and poetic book about it, *The World of Silence*. The book is usually out of print, but it is worth a passionate search.

Mary says only one word, really—*fiat*, "yes". The rest is listening and, therefore, silence.

If you converse with someone who is more ignorant than you, it is best for them if you do most of the talking. If you converse with someone who is much wiser than you, it is best for you if you let him do most of the talking. If you converse with a dumb beast, you have to do all of the talking. (Although the beast may express feelings, it cannot speak truths.) If you converse with God, you should let Him do all or almost all of the talking. For the gap between us and God, which is infinite, is even greater than the gap between us and the beasts, which is finite.

One is silent when one is humble. "Know-it-alls" have to do all the talking. Without humility there is no wisdom, because without humility, there is no listening, and without listening, there is no wisdom.

Kierkegaard said, in many different places, that "If I were allowed to prescribe one remedy for all the ills of the modern world, I would prescribe silence. For even if the Word of God is proclaimed, we do not hear it; there is too much noise. Therefore, first create silence."

As a faithful, pious, and obedient Jew, Mary listened silently to Scripture and to her Sacred Tradition. She also listened, with the unique sensitivity of a mother, to the needs and sufferings of her Son and of her family and her friends and the world around her. She also listened to God's angel. And she also listened to the always-providential and never-accidental but often-puzzling and mysterious events of her life. She was a good Jesuit, finding God in all things. Finally, she listened, as His daughter, to her Heavenly Father in prayer.

We should imitate her silent listening in all of these areas of our lives. Our wisdom will become more like hers in quality and will increase in quantity to the degree that we imitate her.

6. "Pondering"

Twice it is said that Mary kept and "pondered" in her heart the things that were said or done to her (in Lk 2:19 and, implicitly, in vs. 51). What is "pondering", and how does it qualify as a method for finding wisdom?

Pondering is the natural fruit of questioning. (I mean pondering both the question and the answer, insofar as we have one.) Pondering is also itself a further and deeper form of questioning. But it is different in at least two ways from ordinary questioning.

In the first place, it is in the heart, in intuition and feeling, more than in the head, by reasoning and analysis and calculation. In that way, it is like adoration. But it is not, like adoration, merely the receptive contemplation of something known, but it is the active wondering about something unknown. (These two activities, by the way, are not only compatible, but they foster each other, and they also can occur at the same time.)

Second, pondering is a questioning that is solitary. It does not question another; it questions oneself. If the other is God, however, and if God lives in the ponderer's soul, it is a questioning of God and also of oneself, His image. God is not only outside the soul but also inside it. In fact, as Saint Augustine says, God "is more intimately present to me than I am to myself". He transcends both the objective universe and our subjective thoughts. He is not a part of either, yet is totally present to both.

"Pondering" is not only questioning but also contemplating, which is simply a fancy word for looking, in a deep and patient way. Mary's "pondering" has been imitated and exemplified by the Church's patient, millennia-long "pondering" of the data in her Scripture and her Sacred Tradition given to her by Christ and His apostles, whereby she has discovered and appreciated many precious truths about Mary, inspired by the very-much-alive Holy Spirit, Who is "the soul of the Church". Mary's pondering has also been imitated and exemplified by billions of Catholics who have meditated on the mysteries of the Rosary. So if you want to know what Mary's "pondering" was like, you have two contemporary, living examples of it: the Church's deep Marian tradition, crystallized in her Marian dogmas, and your own mind's gradual, subtle deepening in wisdom over the years you have said the Rosary with heart and mind as well as lips. Even weak hearts and minds find great strength and wisdom through praying the Rosary.

For one who knows God experientially, pondering is a natural form of prayer, even when it is not explicitly a prayer. The purposes of prayer are traditionally divided into five: adoration, thanksgiving, confession, intercession, and petition. Perhaps we should add a sixth: pondering.

The questioning in pondering is the opposite of doubt, dismissal, or disdain. One takes the time and effort to ponder only what one knows or believes is deeply important and respected. One does not ponder paper clips.

Pondering is not in tension with "thy will be done" but it is one of the forms it takes. For God deliberately gave us the instinct of what we can call good curiosity. Jesus began His public ministry with a question, one that demands that we question ourselves. It was "What do you seek?" (Jn 1:38). Jesus, like Socrates and the rabbis, loved questions. That was what He was doing in the Temple at twelve with the rabbis, asking and answering questions (Lk 2:46). He was like a duck who had found his natural water. He was so drawn to it that He forgot all about His family. There is not a single example in the Gospels of Jesus discouraging a question from His disciples, no matter how dumb the question was. And they asked some really dumb ones: see Acts 1:6.

Part of "pondering" is *repeating*, walking through the same mental paths over and over, like a cow chewing its cud. This includes both repeating the *question* (e.g., "What are you doing to me, God?") and also repeating the *answers* already known or believed that seem to bear on the question or situation that worries us, e.g., "I know that You are all-wise and never make mistakes and that you are the all-powerful Creator and Designer of everything, including me, and that you are all-good and all-loving to me, and therefore You must be giving me a great good, because that is what love does, but this does not look like good and like love to me now."

We are incredibly forgetful. Our souls are like sieves. The sand seeps out almost as fast as it comes in. We need to re-mind (literally, *re-mind*) ourselves of what we already know. Re-minding is like re-winding a clock. For we are constantly keeping bad time, either too slow and lazy or too fast and jumpy. We all have spiritual ADD, Attention Deficit Disorder. The habit is like a nervous rabbit hopping and scampering away after every second of stillness. It is ridiculously easy for the Devil to hassle our minds. The world's greatest philosopher is easily distracted from his most profound thoughts by a little flea. We keep losing our mind, as a child loses a ball, and we have to keep calling it back.

Aquinas says that the only way to combat a bad habit is by a good habit. So we have to cultivate remembering, over and over again, to combat our forgetting over and over again. We are not angels who make just one choice in eternity and forever with total awareness and free choice. Romeo does not say "I love you" to Juliet once for all, and the Jewish and Christian disciples of King David do not pray his psalms one time only, and Catholics do not say just one Hail Mary but make a big bouquet of roses of them. Muslims say that the origin of all evil is *ghaflah*, forgetting God. That is why they pray five times a day: to scrape off the rust of forgetfulness that keeps accumulating on the soul. That was also Alexandr Solzhenitsyn's wonderfully simple and accurate diagnosis of the origin of all the ills and evils of our modern Western civilization in his great Harvard Commencement Address of 1978: "We have forgotten God."

And even when we do remember, we only half remember and are only half there and half elsewhere, distracted. The saints do not have this spiritual ADD. Or, if they do, it is overcome by the contrary habit of the practicing of His presence all day. I realized this when I met Mother Teresa once, for just about five seconds, at our local parish church. She greeted a few hundred people, one at a time, and when my turn came, she and I were totally alone in the cosmos for a few seconds. All the other space and time in the universe fell away. Nothing else existed for her but me. That is how God's attention is: total. With the totality of His infinite attention He looks at you, and you alone, at every moment. And when great saints get a little closer to that and manifest it in their relation to others, it changes the very nature of time itself. When we give God even a little of our time— say, five loaves and two fishes of it—He miraculously multiplies it.

Contemplative pondering is a little like that: it ignores time. It dares to live in the only real time that ever exists, namely, the present. The rest of us spend most of our lives living in the dead past or the unborn future. Or rather trying to, for we can live in those two unreal times only in our mind. The only time we can really live in is the present.

Jews habitually "pondered" the Law. God's Law was His wonderfully impossible *koan* puzzle for us. We find it hard to understand how they so love to ponder the Law. What a waste of time such meditation seems to be to the busy, worldly utilitarians we have all become! They do it "day and night" (Ps 1), forgetting time. More than that, they *love* the Law that shows us up as fools and sinners. Why? The answer is that the Law is a description of what we are destined for in eternity. It is Messianic; a prophet; a prefiguration of Christ. It is the picture of spiritual beauty that we get in the "Song of Songs" when the bridegroom (God) says to His bride (us) "You are all fair, my love; there is no flaw in you" (Song 4:7). But how can God truly say this to us sinners? Because He sees us end-on, so to speak, like looking at the point of an arrow from the viewpoint of the bull's eye. He looks at our whole life in time from His viewpoint in eternity, as finished and perfected. Mary and the saints subconsciously have more of this divine vision of eternity in time. It is a great grace. And Mary is "full" of this grace, as of all grace.

7. *The Inner Life*

Mary's wisdom welled up from within, not just from without, because she knew that her "within" was the divine farmer's field, the crop, the fruit, the effect, of the same cause, the same God, as the "without" of nature and of her sacred Jewish tradition as well as of all the providential events of her life. These four things (God, nature, her tradition, and her life) meshed in her mind to make a single four-color picture. Her intellect, like her womb, was fructified by the same inner fertilizer of the Holy Spirit. In offering up her lesser fertility by her vow of virginity, she received a far greater fertility from her Divine Spouse.

Jacques Maritain writes, in his essay on "The Preconscious Life of the Intellect", that "far beneath the sunlit surface thronged with explicit concepts and judgments, words and expressed resolutions or movements of the will, are the sources of knowledge and creativity, of love and suprasensuous desires, hidden in . . . the inner abyss of personal freedom." This is the most ourselves *and* the most God, at once, for, as Augustine famously said, God is "more intimately present to us than we are to ourselves".

The universe is outside us. By our bodies we are outside ourselves in the universe. By our souls we are inside ourselves. God is neither inside us, as part of our souls (God is not a thought or a feeling), or outside us, as part of the universe (God is not a planet or a galaxy). God is outside our outside, as the transcendent Creator of the universe. God is also inside our inside, as Augustine saw. He is the supernatural life of our souls as our souls are the life of our bodies. He is the very Life of our life. "Our inner life" means ultimately, not our own self-consciousness but God's gift of life to that very self-consciousness. Mary would not have put that truth in those abstract terms but she knew it by experience.

The inner world of the soul or spirit is as real as the outer world of matter, and at least as active and as dramatic. There are spiritual events as well as physical events. (That is why great "psychological" novels like Dostoyevsky's are even more dramatic than great "thrillers" like *Frankenstein* or *Dracula*.) Both of our two "worlds" are in time, though only the physical world is in space. God is the First, Uncaused Cause of everything in time: of all events spiritual as well as physical, of the events in our inner lives as well as the events in nature. The difference is that the inner events are interpreted and colored by our own minds and some are collaborated with or resisted by our own wills.

We all have a soul and, therefore, an interiority, an inner life. It is a power or potentiality in all of us; it was actualized most perfectly in Mary.

There can be no wisdom without an inner life, as there can be no plant without soil. Most modern Americans do not even know there is such a thing as an "inner life". Why? Paradoxically, part of the answer is that they worry too much about themselves. They look at "mirror, mirror on the wall" and see themselves as "the fairest one of all". But that judgment is reserved for God's eyes. To claim it for your own eyes is our modern idolatry—and a more dangerous form of it than the worship of wood or stone idols, because it is disguised as wisdom and love (it is supposed to be "nonjudgmental", after all). The difference between a real and a fake inner life is the difference between wisdom and folly, between asking God and telling God the two most important things we need to know: who we are and who He is.

I think the most spiritually pornographic and obscene thing I ever heard was the theme song of "The Electric Company", a TV show for little kids (Satan loves to corrupt the innocent as early as possible): "The most important person in the whole wide world is you!" If they bite that bait, they will probably waste half their lives worshipping electronically graven images of themselves on Facebook, and that song will eventually morph into "I Did It My Way", which is the sinister song that summarizes the life of everyone who enters Hell. (Yes, the pun is deliberate. The name

"Sinatra" is close to the French word *sinistre*, means "sinister". It also means "left". I make no political pronouncements here, just puns.)

God is waiting to be invited to sit on your soul's inner throne. He is waiting for you get off His seat.

8. *Openness to Grace*

Of course, the primary and first cause of Mary's wisdom was a special and supernatural gift of divine grace, which began in her Immaculate Conception and continued throughout everything in her life. Grace is, of course, a divine gift, and a divine gift, of course, comes only from the divine Giver; but it is not an "of course" but a divine act of free choice that this divine Giver respects our free will, gives only to those who ask, and gives in proportion to our asking, willing, wanting, loving, and opening our soul, as the hose gives water in proportion to our opening the faucet handle. A gift, after all, is not a gift if it is not both freely given and freely received. That is the only reason why there is a Hell. God freely chooses to give Himself to all; not all freely choose to receive Him. God does not force Himself upon us. He is a spiritual lover, not a spiritual rapist. He is God the Father, not the Godfather who makes you an answer you *can't* refuse.

The supernatural origin of wisdom is clear in the story of how it came to King Solomon, the biblical archetype of wisdom. Mary's wisdom is like Solomon's in its nature, in its divine source, and in her human love of it. We see all three in Solomon's story, which is in essence Mary's story, too:

The LORD appeared to Solomon in a dream by night; and God said, "Ask what I shall give you." And Solomon said, "You have shown great and merciful love to your servant David my father, because he walked before you in faithfulness, in righteousness, and in uprightness of heart toward you; and you have kept for him this great and merciful love, and have given him a son to sit on his throne this day. And now, O LORD my God, you have made your servant king in place of David my father, although I am but a little child; I do not know how to go out or come in. And your servant is in the midst of your people whom you have chosen, a great people, that cannot be numbered or counted for multitude. Give your servant therefore an understanding mind to govern your people, that I may discern between good and evil; for who is able to govern this great people of yours?"

It pleased the LORD that Solomon had asked this. And God said to him, "Because you have asked this, and have not asked for yourself long life or riches or the life of your enemies, but have asked for yourself understanding to discern what is right, behold, I now do according to your word. Behold, I give you a wise and discerning mind, so that none like you has been before you and none like you shall arise after you. I give you also what you have not asked, both riches and honor, so that no other king shall compare with you, all your days." (1 Kings 3:5–13)

This was the way to wisdom that Solomon modeled for all subsequent Jews. For instance, the anonymous writer of the first century B.C. deuterocanonical "Wisdom of Solomon":

Therefore I prayed, and understanding was given me;
  I called upon God, and the spirit of wisdom came to
    me [compare Lk 1:35].
I preferred her to scepters and thrones,

and I accounted wealth as nothing in comparison with
   her.
Neither did I liken to her any priceless gem,
because all gold is but a little sand in her sight,
and silver will be accounted as clay before her.
I loved her more than health and beauty,
and I chose to have her rather than light,
because her radiance never ceases.
All good things came to me along with her . . .
she was their mother. (Wis 7:7–12)

9. Closeness to Christ

It is a simple syllogism. Mary is the Mother of God Incarnate, the second Person of the Trinity. He is the *Logos*, the Word of God, the Mind of God, the Wisdom of God, Wisdom Itself. Therefore Mary is Wisdom's mother.

"Mother" is the closest relationship any two human beings can have to each other. In fact, for the first nine months of your life, you did not even know there was any distinction between you and your mother.

Jesus' apostles knew Him better than any other men did, except Saint Joseph, his foster father. Yet the apostles had at least three very practical limitations that Mary did not have. (1) They knew Him with fallen, sinful, clouded minds. They were not immaculately conceived without Original Sin. The mental consequences of that moral fact are immense. (2) They knew Him for only the three years of His public ministry. And (3) they knew Him only as His friends and disciples.

But Mary (1) knew Him with an unfallen and unclouded mind. (2) She knew Him for thirty-three years and nine months, through all the stages of His life, preborn and born, infant, youth, teenager, and adult. (3) And she knew Him as only a mother can know her son. How much more wisdom must she have imbibed from His spiritual and physical closeness, as He imbibed milk from her breasts!

Wisdom is not an abstract idea. Wisdom is a concrete individual Divine Person (see 1 Cor 1:24, 30). No one was ever closer to this Person than Mary, either in body or in soul. That is the deepest reason why Mary had such unparalleled wisdom.

This is also God's prescription for our wisdom. We, too, can share Mary's wisdom because we can share some of her closeness to Christ both in spirit and even in body. In spirit, like her, through our faith and hope and love of Christ— and this is possible because He has given us His Spirit—and also in body, because He has given us, not just His mind, but His own Body in the Eucharist.

It is done by divine grace, of course, not by human effort. Yet it is not done without human effort, because grace loves and perfects and uses nature, human nature, and free will.

Unlike us, Mary was "*full* of grace". But it is the same grace that is in us, even though in lesser proportion, since what we are more likely to be full of is *skubala*. Yet God even uses our *skubala*, like all *skubala*, as fertilizer! (I owe this delightful image to Matt Fradd.)

Mary is totally transparent to Christ, like a clear window to the light. She always looks to Him and points us to Him. We are meant to look along her pointing fingers and eyes, rather than to be satisfied with looking *at* them, like a dog only sniffing the finger that is pointing to its food. She is like a pointer dog, stretching out her whole body, head to tail, toward the prey that we need to capture and eat, which is the love of Christ.

10. Virginity

Mary's virginity was another cause of her wisdom. Of course, not every virgin is wise, and not every wise person is a virgin. But the connection between virginity and wisdom is a natural one, not an accidental one. And it works both ways: her wisdom caused her to choose virginity, and her virginity was a cause of her wisdom.

The first of those two causal connections (wisdom causing virginity) can be seen if we look at two questions Christ asked. One was the very first thing He said in John's Gospel, to His future disciples: "What do you seek [want, love]?" (Jn 1:38). He asked the same question to Saint Thomas Aquinas in a vision when He said to him after he had finished the section of his *Summa* on the Eucharist: "You have written well of Me, Thomas; what will you have as your reward?" Thomas, Mary, and Jesus' disciples all gave the same answer: "Only Yourself, Lord."

Because Mary wanted only her Lord, she renounced marriage, sex, and children—all very great goods. Virginity, of course, presupposes that sex is a great good, not evil, dirty, or low; for it is an insult to offer up to God anything but the very best. She had fallen totally in love with God, and that is the essence of sanctity and of wisdom. The reason we are not saints is our reluctance to say the first word of Saint Thomas' answer to Christ, the word "only".

Not only does wisdom cause and choose virginity, but virginity is also a cause, or at least an aid, to wisdom. The reason is obvious. All the premodern sages, pagan as well as Christian, observed the obvious fact that sex blinds the mind. We moderns are the first either to deny or to ignore that fact (or perhaps we just don't care about our mind any more): the fact that it is rather difficult to contemplate truth objectively while in the throes of sexual passion.

Sex is also addictive, since it is the most pleasurable of bodily activities. No one becomes addicted to cleaning belly button lint. The pleasure is God's design, of course, Who wisely attached the most delicious carrot to the greatest stick, to the most powerful deed we can do, namely, the miracle of the procreation of a human being.

Sexual desire also fosters the most rationalization, and rationalization is reason's greatest enemy, far more powerful and deadly than ignorance. We deeply want to justify what we most deeply want. We thus play God, the author and teacher of truth rather than its obedient student. Today we go so far as to speak of "my" truth versus "your" truth, as if truth were a pet on a leash. We never descend to such insanity when we do science but do so only when we rationalize our sexual desires and deeds.

Saint Thomas Aquinas acquired a supernatural freedom from this diversion from wisdom when he received a supernatural gift of chastity from God after he resisted his brothers' attempt to seduce him out of his vocation with a prostitute by driving her out of his prison cell with a burning brand, and God did the same thing to his natural lust. He gave him a clarity of mind unsurpassed in history among philosophers.

No one ever had more of this clarity than Mary.

11. *Innocence*

Mary's immaculate innocence gave her a wisdom not only about good but also about evil. The sober know what drunkenness is and what it does much better than drunks do, and the sane know insanity better than the insane do. Similarly, saints know vice as well as virtue better than sinners do.

Innocence is not naïveté. In *The Passion of the Christ*, on the *via dolorosa* to Calvary, Mary is the only one who sees Satan, meeting him eye to eye. Some things are known best from a distance—like tornadoes. Other things are known best by intimacy—like spouses. Heaven understands Hell far better than Hell understands itself. That is why we will have to wait until we are in Heaven, and are heavenly, to understand Hell. Saints understand sinners (and themselves) better than sinners understand saints (or themselves). That is why Mary is the most effective "refuge of sinners": because she understands sinners better than anyone else does except Christ.

But Satan is a clever liar, and he has deceived most of us with the lie that evil makes you wise. The first example of that was in the Garden of Eden, when he persuaded Eve to eat the forbidden fruit so that she could become "like God, knowing good and evil" (Gen 3:5). But knowing evil (by experience) means NOT knowing good. God does not "know" evil by experience, from within, as we do. He has no "dark side", and it is the very simplicity of His goodness that gives Him a total understanding of evil. He knows (*savoir, wissen*) evil best because He knows (*connaître, kennen*) no evil. Of all mere creatures, Mary has the most of that innocence and, therefore, that wisdom.

But is there not also a kind of knowledge of evil, and of insanity and drunkenness and addiction and misery and death, that comes only by experience? Is the absence of that kind of knowledge not a lack in the innocent? No, for this "knowledge" is not knowledge at all but ignorance. It is "knowledge" only in the sense that it is felt, like pain. Experiencing evil casts no new light on good but only steals away the light we had. (An example of that principle is the cynic's conviction that "everybody has his price", in other words, everyone is like him; there are no saints, only fools, liars, and hypocrites.)

12. Faith

We will not get wisdom unless we love it and fight for it, and we will not love it and fight for it unless we hope to attain it. And we will not hope for it without faith. What generates this hope is faith, for hope is faith's extension into the future. It all begins with faith. And Mary is a hero and paradigm of faith.

Faith is the root of the whole plant that is our religion, i.e., our relationship with God. Faith is our first connecting link to the God who is our mind's source of truth, our will's source of good, and our heart's source of beauty and life and joy. Faith has these three dimensions because it fulfills our three distinctively human powers of the soul: the mind, the will, and the heart. The three dimensions of faith are, respectively, belief in the mind, obedience in the will and action, and trust in the heart and feelings. Belief is an act of the mind; obedience is an act of the will; and trust is an act of the heart.

The three are not necessarily always in that chronological order. Trust usually comes first, because if we do not trust someone, we are reluctant to believe him or obey him.

Belief and obedience depend on each other and stand or fall together. When we begin to disobey God's will, we begin to lose the belief dimension of our faith; and when we begin to lose the belief aspect of our faith, we begin to disobey. This is because the mind and the will depend on each other and stand or fall together. The will commands the mind to think or not to think, and the mind tells the will what to command and what not to command. The will is the soul's captain, and the mind is its navigator. They depend on each other.

Belief, obedience, and trust are three dimensions of faith, not three stages of faith. They always grow or decline together. For "dimensions" are different only in the abstract; they are abstract aspects of a single concrete thing, namely, the individual person. Mind, will, and heart are three different *powers* of the single person, and belief, obedience, and trust are *dimensions* of a single faith.

Mary models all three dimensions of faith for us:

(1) Mary *trusts* God; that is, she *entrusts* herself, totally, body and soul, to God. For trust is not only a feeling but also a willing, a choice to "bank" on God, to "entrust" one's whole self to God's First Supernatural Bank and Trust Company. (a) Mary is totally faithful to God and to her vow to Him, (b) to Joseph and to her vow to him, and (c) to her divinely given task regarding her divine Child and to her vow to fulfill this mission, this vocation. No one else ever needed a greater trust because no one ever had a greater vocation.

(2) Mary *believes* in God: not just in His existence, but also in His trustability, which is grounded in His omniscience, omnipotence, and omnibenevolence; His infinite wisdom, power, and love. Faith (in its dimension of belief), according to the classic *Baltimore Catechism*, is "an act of the intellect, prompted by the will, by which we believe everything God has revealed on the grounds of the authority of the One Who revealed it, Who can neither deceive nor be deceived."

(3) Mary, therefore, *obeys* God. Obedience is not only the effect or outcome or expression of faith; it is also faith itself in action, as the fruit is the plant itself in its consummation. The great chapter in Scripture on the heroes of faith,

Hebrews 11, repeatedly says that "by faith" these heroes acted, did, worked, obeyed. The Hebrew word *emeth* is often translated as "faith" but more often as "fidelity" (which is faithful *actions*), and sometimes as "truth". Faith, in its consummation, is "*doing* the truth". Truth (in the Hebrew language) is *done*, truth *happens*. It is not just in thought; it is also in action.

All this is included, in embryo, in the "fear of God" that "is the beginning of wisdom". Mary's *fiat* expresses all three dimensions of faith as perfectly and as succinctly as possible. Faith is not a state of soul that we work up inside ourselves; it is essentially relational and other-directed, a response to divine revelation. "God said it, I believe it; that settles it." Saints say that. Saints are profound enough to be simple.

13. Obedience

The most important things in life cannot be understood with the mind unless we first do them with our will and our bodies. Wisdom is one of these things. It depends on obedience.

That is true in science as well as in religion. In science, obedience means obeying the facts, judging all theories by data, by a kind of obedience to the world as known by sensory experience. It also means obedience to all the known laws that govern the science, e.g., the laws of mathematics, of logic, of physics, of biology, etc. Francis Bacon points out that we habitually err by imposing theories onto data, prejudices onto experience, our own neat little orderings and expectations onto nature.

And we do that even more to other people. Other people surprise us because they shatter our simplistic stereotypes of them. This is the major obstacle to communication. They say x, and we reply, "What I hear you saying is. . . ." And then we say y.

Most of all, we do this to God. Voltaire said, "God created man in His own image, and ever since, man has been returning that compliment."

Christ gave us His practical method for wisdom, in John 7:17. To the Jews who did not understand His teaching and who did not believe it came from God, He said: "if any man's will is to do his will, he shall know whether the teaching is from God or whether I am speaking on my own authority." To understand God's mind, we must do God's will. To understand the map, we must use it; we must make the journey and obey the instructions.

Mary was obedient to God's angel. Christ Himself was totally obedient to His Father (Jn 4:34) and to His parents (Lk 2:51).

Mary understood that obedience is not demeaning but liberating, because we are not God and we have been placed into various hierarchies of authority by God: religious, familial, and civic. Our Declaration of Independence paradoxically bases our right to liberty on the fact that we are not at the top of the hierarchy, that we have been "endowed by our Creator" with our rights. On this "subordination" is based our right to rebellion against any state that pretends to be a God over us, the Author of our rights.

Obedience can be grounded in either fear or love and trust. Love and trust *want* to surrender to the Beloved. "Free love", as Chesterton points out, is a contradiction in terms. Lovers want to be bound to each other and, therefore, to their word, their promises, their obedience, not to be free from each other. Saint Paul's admonition was to "be servants of [obedient to] one another" (Gal 5:13).

Mary's first words in Scripture are her obedience to God's angel and her last words tell us (the waiters at Cana) to obey her Son ("Do whatever he tells you.") This is the highest wisdom. When I was about eight, I said to my father, "Dad, all this stuff they teach us in church and Sunday School, it all comes down to just one thing, doesn't it? You just have to ask God what He wants you to do, and then do it, right?" I still remember my father's smile in admiration of my child-like wisdom. Unfortunately, it has all been downhill since that moment.

Fulton Sheen says (in the world's best book about Mary, *The World's First Love*), "Our Lord spent three hours in redeeming, three years in teaching, and thirty years in obeying."

Mary is so most profoundly and totally wise because she is so most profoundly and totally obedient. Her "yes", her "amen", her *fiat* to God, is the one-word secret of wisdom.

14. Accepting Suffering

"The man who has not suffered—what can he possibly know, anyway?" asked Rabbi Abraham Joshua Heschel. Even the ancient pagans knew that. Aeschylus wrote: "Hour by hour, pain drips upon the heart, as even in our own despite comes wisdom from the awful grace of the god." Charles Williams spoke of "a terrible good". C. S. Lewis spoke of Aslan, Narnia's Christ, as both "terrible" and "good". Sheldon Vanauken spoke of suffering and death as God's "severe mercy". Such paradoxical juxtapositions as "awful" and "grace", "terrible" and "good", "severe" and "mercy", seem to contradict each other. But the wise perceive that they do not.

This wisdom sees suffering as a high thing, not a low thing; a holy task, a calling, a mission, a vocation from God, not a mistake and a tragedy. For a Christian, all suffering can be like Christ's Passion and death in that way if it is offered up as a participation in His Passion by a Christian who is a member of His Body which is the Church.

Many people, and even many Christians, see Christ's Passion and death as a tragedy. They are profoundly wrong. It was a life-saving operation. It was the operation that *healed* the tragedy. It accomplished the greatest good and even the greatest joy, in the end: the salvation of those He loved. Christ "for the joy that was set before him endured the cross, despising the shame" (Heb 12:2).

When the prophet Simeon, at the Presentation, told Mary that a sword would pierce her soul (Lk 2:35), she accepted this as a necessary part of her task from God, who she knew was all loving, not just from Fate or Necessity, or even from a God who was all-wise and all-holy and all-just and all-righteous, but perhaps not all-merciful and all-compassionate and all-tender to His children. That is the Stoic heresy, and Mary absolutely repudiated that with just as much decisiveness as she repudiated the opposite heresy, the one that denied God's omnipotence and omniscience and saw Him as a compassionate big brother who was on our side and did all He could, but it wasn't enough. That latter heresy is especially tempting when someone we love experiences horrible suffering and apparent tragedy and loss, as happened to Rabbi Kushner, author of *When Bad Things Happen to Good People*. His son had progeria, which gives you a ninety-year-old body before you are nineteen. The rabbi's solution was to deny God's omnipotence in order to preserve His love and compassion.

But an even worse event, which even more strongly

seemed to be a "tragedy", namely crucifixion, also happened to another, wiser father: to God the Father, who loved His Son infinitely more than any human being did, even Mary. Yet He allowed this. In fact, He planned it. And the sword of this same kind of suffering also pierced the heart of Mary. Christ was her only begotten Son temporally just as truly as He was His Father's only begotten Son eternally.

Actively accepting suffering as a God-given task transforms suffering from passivity into activity. This can also be done with death. In death, we can actively offer up our entire life to God, like an author sending his completed book to the printer. Although death itself is not avoidable, merely suffering it passively as a tragedy *is* avoidable. Christ said: "I lay down my life. . . . No one takes it from me, but I lay it down of my own accord" (Jn 10:17–18). The same can be true for us, though not in the same way as it was for Christ. Our crosses are only tiny splinters of His. But we, too, can actually pick them up and carry them as He did and participate in His act if we participate in His Body.

Everything (except sin) comes from God's love; therefore, suffering does, too. Love takes mysterious forms. Love sometimes sees in us the potential for heroism and a high and holy joy in the end and, therefore, gives us tasks that seem far too hard for us. But God makes no mistakes.

But how can a loving Father will that his children suffer?

There are four possible ways God can will a thing. In two of these senses, He does, and in two, He does not will our sufferings.

(1) He directly wills our holiness, our sanctity, our *fiat* to Him, our conformity with His will, our free choice of faith and hope and love, which are the way to our holiness and deepest happiness, even though it requires suffering on the way. So He wills our suffering indirectly, as a necessary

part of the whole "package deal". That holy *fiat* both from Mary and from us is to His plan, not our own. Our own never includes suffering; His does.

(2) He also directly wills our deepest happiness and joy, which are the outcome of our holiness, which requires suffering.

(3) He does not directly will, want, or love our pain. But He allows it, He permits it, thus He indirectly wills our sufferings, as loving parents will the sufferings of their children by bringing them into this world. He did not create or invent those sufferings. They are the result of the Fall. They are the inevitable consequence of our sins, though not in a one-to-one way, as Job's three friends wrongly thought. Our body and soul are so one (like the words and the meaning of a book) that when either soul or body falls, the other does, too. When our soul fell away from God by sin, our body fell away from our soul, producing suffering and death. When we pulled the plug to God, in Eden, we pulled the plug both to holiness and happiness, because they are tied together in an eternally necessary "package deal". We suffer because we sin, first collectively in Adam in Eden and then individually in the millions of echoes of that original noise that resound in our present lives.

But God uses these physical evils of suffering and death, though they were invented by us and the Devil, not God, as the best way to our eventual ultimate holiness and therefore happiness, and we will see this and thank Him for it in Heaven, though we do not see it now and can only thank Him by faith here below. That has been the consistent teaching of the Bible, the Church, and all the Jewish and Christian saints and sages.

(4) God does not will us to sin, either directly or indi-

rectly; in fact, He wills us not to sin. But He foresees our sins and allows them to exist by refusing to destroy our free will, which would be the only way to prevent them. More, He uses even our sins, through the golden door of repentance, for our greater good, like a jazz musician improvising the way to turn a wrong note into a right note or a sculptor using an imperfection like a crack in his marble to make an even more beautiful statue (perhaps a lightning bolt).

The alternative to seeing our apparent tragedies as part of God's perfect plan for our lives is to lose our faith, either in God's love or in His wisdom or in His power. It is hard to have faith in a God who is even a little unloving, a little unwise, or a little weak—for instance, a God who is the Author and Designer, not of our whole lives, but only of the nice parts. Mary's wisdom knew all this—in fact, she knew it so well that she did not need to formulate it in theological terms as I have done—and that is why she accepted her sword of seven sorrows. They were and are her strongest weapon in her spiritual warfare for us and against our Enemy, as Christ's Cross is His. His Cross is the sword with which He defeats the Devil.

It is no accident that the Cross is shaped like an upside-down sword, held at the hilt by the hand of Heaven and plunged into the flesh of the earth, not to kill, but to heal, not to take our blood, like Dracula, but to give us His blood, like a transfusion. Salvation is a blood transfusion. It is given to us in the Eucharist. The altar is our operating table.

Fulton Sheen and Saint John Paul II say two things about suffering that I found extremely positive, though many find them extremely negative: (1) "God wants you to suffer" (Sheen) and (2) "Don't waste your suffering" (Pope John Paul II). The reason for both sayings is that suffering is spiritually powerful when accepted and offered up in faith. If we freely offer it up to God, He will certainly use it for greater good than we can see.

This can be a wonderfully liberating thought and can transform our suffering from intolerable to not just tolerable but mysteriously wonderful, something for which to be grateful. Of course, as Job discovered, the gratitude for it is much easier after it ceases. But it is possible, and precious and powerful, even before.

Christ came, not to remove our sufferings, but to transform them. If this is not so, then He was a failure, especially compared to Buddha. Buddhism claims to save us from suffering, not from sin. In fact, Buddha saved us from suffering by denying the very idea of sin, the very idea that there is a real, substantial self behind our desires and willings, a self that is the responsible cause of both good and evil by its free will. If there is no self there is no selfish desire, and therefore no frustration of desire, which is what suffering is. Christ came to save us, not from self or from suffering, but from sin, and He did it precisely by means of suffering. And He does, today, in our lives, a little bit of the very same thing that He did in His own day in His own life.

The alternative to these two controversial points is to see suffering as NOT part of God's loving, caring, merciful, and tender plan and will for our lives, as something outside His control. Which means that there is no such being as God the omnipotent and omniscient Creator and Designer of the entire universe. There is no tenable third option, no compromise between that holiness and that heresy, between Mary's *fiat* and atheism. A nice God, a tame God, a tolerable God, a human God, a weak, wicked, or wobbly God is a self-contradiction. There is no other God. The Muslims are right: "There is no God but God."

That is all true. On the other hand, it is also true that most thoughtful and sensitive Christians who work in children's hospitals are outraged at the thought that God wants these beautiful, courageous, innocent children to suffer and die. They are tempted to think that they have to abandon either the idea that God is tender and loving and caring and merciful or the idea that God is all-powerful and all-wise. They have a hard task: to endure and not to deny either of these two things that seem to contradict each other. And the worst thing of all to give up is the faith that God is love. That is clearly contradicted by the Word of God in both senses of that term: Scripture and Christ, the word of God on paper and the Word of God on wood, the wood of the Cross. God's power and wisdom, by contrast, though clearly taught as true, are much more mysterious, transcendent, and unknowable to us than His love. So while it is not permissible to deny God's omnipotence or omniscience, as Rabbi Kushner did, it is understandable. And it is perfectly permissible to doubt my philosophical and theological solution to the problem of suffering and simply to accept humbly all the divinely revealed data, including God's omnipotence and omniscience, but to put all your faith and focus and confidence in His love—especially when dealing with children, especially your own. In fact I think that is what Mary did.

~

"Suffering" means two things: (1) the wax "suffers" the seal objectively, both physically and metaphysically (ontologically), and (2) the soul "suffers" sorrow subjectively, psychologically and emotionally. Mary suffers the most psychologically because she suffers the most ontologically; she suffers the most sorrow because she is "suffering" or receiving Christ the most.

~

If you knew anything about philosophy today, you were probably surprised by this whole chapter, because every one of these principles of Mary's methodology is not impersonal and scientific but personal. This is because true philosophy, the love of wisdom, is personal, since both love and wisdom are personal. Wisdom cannot be stored on a computer, as knowledge can. Philosophers have always disagreed, and always will, unlike scientists, because although data and argument can be shared, wisdom cannot. But when most philosophers today think of method, they think of something impersonal, like the instructions for assembling a machine.

Chapter II

MARY'S EPISTEMOLOGY

Epistemology is the philosophy of knowing. "Knowing" has three different levels. The first two are distinguished in most languages, but not in English: *wissen* and *kennen* in German; *savoir* and *connaître* in French. The first is impersonal knowledge of a fact from without. The second is personal knowledge of a person from within, i.e., by sharing the same nature ("connaturality") with that person, either simply by membership in the same species or by a more personal similarity of character. Obviously, when it comes to science, the first is superior. Knowing how the body works in an objective and universal way, by anatomy and physiology, will enable you to do surgery better than knowing it simply by living in a body. But when it comes to knowing *persons*, obviously the second kind of knowing is more adequate. That is the point of Michael Polanyi's titles *Personal Knowledge* and *The Tacit Dimension* (for personal knowledge is implicit or tacit more often than explicit and defined).

But there is a third and even closer kind of knowing, and in Hebrew it also means sexual intercourse. Thus, in Genesis 3, the "knowledge" of good and evil are a kind of intercourse with evil as well as good; and in Genesis 4, Adam "knew" Eve, and the product was not a book of psychological theory but a baby. It is this third and highest kind of "knowledge" that the saints have. They dare to call it "the spiritual marriage" with Christ. Mary has it preeminently.

97

For most philosophers, epistemology focuses on impersonal knowledge rather than personal knowledge. Its two
main questions are: (1) which of the two poles of our knowing, the sensory or the rational, is prior and (2) whether
knowing means discovery or creation, whether we know
real things as they really are in themselves or whether we
form and shape them in the act of knowing them and can
know only the way they appear to us.

The first issue is the dispute between rationalists, like
Descartes, and empiricists, like Hume. Rationalism claims
that we begin with reason in that we have innate ideas (e.g.,
that x does not equal non-x and that $1 + 1 = 2$); empiricism
claims that all that is in the intellect comes from prior sense
experience. Rationalism also claims that reason must judge
sense experience, while empiricism claims the reverse: that
sense data must judge and prove or disprove theories. So the
issue is one of priority both in time and in authority.

The second issue is the dispute between pre-Kantian and
post-Kantian epistemology, i.e., between epistemological realism and epistemological idealism. Pre-Kantian realists define truth as the conformity of our mind to real objects,
while Kant's "critical idealism" reverses that and claims that
the structures we find in the objects we know are constructed by the mind and that we can know only things-
as-they-appear-to-us (to both mind and senses) rather than
things-as-they-are-in-themselves.

If Mary were to address these two questions, she would
not participate in the debate that has been central to modern philosophy. On the first issue, she begins neither with
reason nor with sense experience but with faith. Implicitly,
this includes faith in God's gifts to human nature of both
reason and sense experience and also her personal faith in the
Giver. On the second issue, she does not ask the question,

much less answer it: like all ordinary people, she assumes epistemological realism and acts as if what she knows is real, not constructed.

But these two answers, or non-answers, that she would give to the two classic questions of epistemology are not distinctively Marian or even distinctively religious. Why does she not address these two questions? They are important, aren't they?

No. Not nearly as important as the question we have already seen her addressing in many concrete ways in the last chapter on practical methodology for attaining wisdom. For —as we have had the need to remind ourselves more than once before—Mary is a true philosopher in the two primary and original senses of the word: the moving force of her philosophy is love, not just curiosity, and its end is wisdom, not just knowledge.

But that means that this chapter will be (mercifully) short and that its main point will be the negative one, a point about a non-point, a justification for an "excused absence", such as a child brings to his teacher. To make this point, however, is also to make the positive point of the priority of the practical question. Both from within herself and from the "without" of her Jewish tradition and Scriptures, which are eminently practical, Mary prioritized the issue of practical wisdom—as she did at Cana, for instance, when she reminded her Son that "they have no wine." What I think she would say about our current philosophical scene is similar: "They have no wisdom." Mary wants to solve the problem, not just define it! She is not like the brilliant doctor at the university to whom Dostoyevsky obliquely refers, in *The Brothers Karamazov*, who can not cure you, but he can tell you exactly what you are dying of.

To many contemporary philosophers, Mary's omission of

theoretical epistemology will be sufficient proof that she is not a philosopher at all. That narrow focus is one of the reasons most academic philosophers are no longer taken very seriously today. They are not *interesting*. Beginning with Descartes' "I think, therefore I am", modern philosophers typically begin with knowledge (and therefore epistemology) and try to deduce being (and metaphysics) from it; to break out of the knowing of knowing (epistemology) into the knowing of being (metaphysics). They do not usually succeed in knowing even a simple thing like a horse. They put Descartes before the horse.

Both the "within" of her motherly instincts and the "without" of her eminently practical Jewish tradition and Scriptures led Mary to concentrate on the practical rather than the theoretical. I strongly suspect that one of her favorite passages of Scripture was Job 28. It is an astonishingly up-to-date passage for our era of improved means to decayed ends, an age in which almost all university research and development money goes to the STEM courses, which deal with efficient technological, scientific, economic, and mathematical means, and only a very small amount to all the arts and all the humanities, which deal with human ends. When you read the following passage from the 28th chapter of the Book of Job, try to hear with your heart as well as your head the contrast between our success at science and technology and our failure at wisdom:

> "Surely there is a mine for silver,
>   and a place for gold which they refine.
> Iron is taken out of the earth,
>   and copper is smelted from the ore.
> Men put an end to darkness,
>   and search out to the farthest bound
>   the ore in gloom and deep darkness [of mines].

They open shafts in a valley away from where men live;
    they are forgotten by travelers,
    they hang afar from men, they swing back and forth.
As for the earth, out of it comes bread;
    but underneath it is turned up as by fire. . . .
"Man puts his hand to the flinty rock,
    and overturns mountains by the roots.
He cuts out channels in the rocks,
    and his eye sees every precious thing.
He binds up the streams so that they do not trickle,
    and the thing that is hidden he brings forth to light.
"But where shall wisdom be found?
    And where is the place of understanding?
Man does not know the way to it,
    and it is not found in the land of the living.
The deep says, 'It is not in me,'
    and the sea says, 'It is not with me.'
It cannot be gotten for gold,
    and silver cannot be weighed as its price. . . .
"From where does wisdom come?
    And where is the place of understanding?
It is hidden from the eyes of all living,
    and concealed from the birds of the air. . . .
"God understands the way to it,
    and he knows its place.
For he looks to the ends of the earth,
    and sees everything under the heavens.
When he gave to the wind its weight,
    and meted out the waters by measure,
when he made a decree for the rain,
    and a way for the lightning of the thunder;
then he saw it and declared it;
    he established it, and searched it out.
And he said to man,
'Behold, the fear of the Lord, that is wisdom;
    and to depart from evil is understanding.'"

~

The thing Job and Solomon and Mary sought, practical wisdom, is called "prudence" in a much older and larger sense than the shriveled contemporary connotation of "safety first". In this older, larger sense, "prudence" is both an intellectual and a moral virtue, according to Plato, Aristotle, Augustine, and Aquinas. It seeks truth both for its own sake (honesty demands that, for the only honest reason for anyone ever to believe anything is that it is true) and also for the sake of life, of practice. Prudence is the first of the four cardinal moral virtues and their foundation, for we cannot attain justice, courage, or temperance unless we know what they are, so that we know what to seek. That is so commonsensical that only a philosopher could possibly forget it.

I think I have said enough to cause something of a sigh of relief in readers who realize that such pretzels of thought, such abstract and theoretical questions as I have found necessary to present in order to introduce the reader to theoretical epistemology in this short chapter, are now mercifully ended. Mary was simply too interested in knowing who God is to be interested in knowing what knowing is. She never got ingrown eyeballs.

Chapter III

MARY'S LOGIC

Oops! (= modern Short Act of Contrition) I lied at the end of the last chapter. Here is one more apparently theoretical and abstract chapter, on logic.

But, to those who know modern philosophy, it will not be the kind of thing Russell and Whitehead mean by logic, but the kind of thing Hegel means by it. In a word, not computation, but dialectic; not mathematical logic, but metaphysical logic. That may make it more mysterious, but at least it is more interesting.

We usually begin teaching philosophy with teaching logic, not because it is the most important division of philosophy, but because it is in one sense the least important. It is a means to further ends. Our ordering of the chapters of this book is similarly progressive, from the most abstract and theoretical, and the most formal and empty of content, to the most concrete and practical and full, which is the philosophy of religion.

Logic is to philosophy as telescope making is to astronomy, or math is to physics: honing the instrument to be subsequently used for serious work. It is a means, not an end. Telescopes would be pointless if there were no images of things like stars that we wanted to magnify.

Logic is usually presented as a set of rules for three structures of thinking: (1) for defining terms, (2) for formulating judgments (propositions), and (3) above all, for evaluating arguments. Mary has nothing to say about this purely formal logic, for the same reason she has nothing to say about mathematics: because it is not controversial. It does not require wisdom. A computer can do it, or at least the third and major part of it. Formal logic is the same in all times, places, and cultures. There is no such thing as Eastern vs. Western logic, or masculine vs. feminine logic, or modern vs. ancient logic, or even wise logic vs. unwise logic, just as there is no such thing as wise or unwise, feminine or masculine, Eastern or Western mathematics. There are only different formulations of it. "All A is B and all B is C, therefore all A is C" is as universal and noncontroversial as "$2 + 2 = 4$." This is theoretical logic, or "formal logic".

But when it comes to practical logic, or "informal logic", there are wiser and less wise ways of ordering our thoughts; and this admits of different degrees or levels of wisdom, although these differences are much less sharp and distinctive in this field of philosophy than in any of the others. Nevertheless, even here we can perceive some Marian wisdom, though it is less unique and distinctive here than in the other divisions of philosophy.

It is probably bad strategy to begin with the weakest case for our controversial conclusion (that Mary is the greatest philosopher) rather than the strongest one. On the other hand, it can constitute an *a fortiori* ("from the stronger") argument: if Mary's wisdom is visible even here, it will be even more visible elsewhere.

~

The most impressive and distinctive feature of the order or structure or form of Mary's thinking is that it usually takes a both-and rather than an either-or form.

A "both-and" often appears as a paradox (i.e., an apparent, but not a real, contradiction). For instance, free will and predestination (or destiny or fate). Every story has both of these two dimensions, even though the two ideas seem to contradict each other. There cannot be a good story about robots, nor can a story be purely random. The characters need to be free, yet predestined by their author. Another example is the paradox of grace and nature, the supernatural (or more than natural) and the natural (or less than supernatural). Both of these are at work in all events. To ask whether it was God who parted the Red Sea or Moses or the "strong east wind all night" is like asking whether it was Socrates, his disciple Plato, or Plato's mind that was responsible for the *Apology*. Or take the paradox that man is "very good" (Gen 1:31, Ps 8:5) and man is "corrupt" (Ps 14:2-3). Both are clearly true and clearly affirmed in Scripture. And even if we try to escape the apparent contradiction by distinguishing between man's ontological goodness and his moral badness, that moral badness is not pure badness. As Thornton Wilder wrote, "There's a bit of good in the worst of us and a bit of bad in the best of us, so it ill becomes the best of us to speak ill of the worst of us."

Most philosophers eschew paradoxes; that is why they tend toward ideological one-sidedness and reductionism. For instance, when it comes to philosophical anthropology, or the philosophy of human nature, we find four possibilities: (1) that man is good ("optimists" like Rousseau), (2) that man is evil ("pessimists" like Calvin and Hobbes and Machiavelli), (3) that man is neither good nor evil (amoralists and moral relativists), and (4) that man is both good and evil. Only the last is paradoxical, and only if it says more than merely that man is partly good and partly evil, only if it says that he is wholly good and wholly evil. And even while pure logic says this is the least likely of the possibilities, our intuitive commonsense wisdom knows that it is true.

A paradox can only be an apparent logical contradiction, not a real one, because reality does not really contradict itself. The simple reason why there cannot be real contradictions is that they are literally meaningless. If I say that I both see the light and do not see the light at the same time, and if I mean the very same thing by "see" and "light" and "I", then I am saying nothing that has any meaning at all. I am saying something meaningful only if I say that I see with my eyes but not with my mind or that I see the light of wisdom but not the light of photons or if I say I see it with my intuitive mind but not with my rational mind. If I say both Yes and No about exactly the same thing, I am saying neither Yes nor No but Yo. But Yo does not mean anything. It is only the guttural sound that Rocky used to greet Adrianne.

Thus, e.g., prophets, who are called "seers", are often blind, like Tiresias in *Oedipus the King*, because he "sees" (understands) the fate that the sighted Oedipus does not "see". Another famous example is Jesus saying to the Pharisees that they are blind precisely because they claim to see (Jn 9:41) and that those who deny that they are spiritually ill are truly spiritually ill (Lk 5:29–32), while those who admit their illness are the only healthy ones (Lk 18:9–14). That paradox is the point of the parable of the Pharisee and the publican (Lk 18:9–14). It was also the point of the Delphic Oracle's paradox about Socrates in Plato's *Apology*, that he was the wisest of men although he knew he had no true wisdom—precisely because he knew that. Socrates taught that there are only two kinds of people: the wise, who know they are fools, and the fools, who think they are wise. Jesus taught that there are only two kinds of people: the saints, who know they are sinners, and the sinners, who think they are saints. The saints are happy because they are unhappy (with their sins), and the sinners are (really, objectively) unhappy because they are (psychologically, subjectively) happy with their sins.

Greek is the language that God providentially provided for the New Testament to be written in. (Ending a sentence with a preposition like that is something up with which we should not put.) Greek is the best language ever invented for philosophy. It has more distinctions and alternative meanings than English does for basic concepts like "love" and "know" and "time", and therefore it is open to the most paradoxes. It also has a crucial set of little words in it (they are called "particles" because they do not fit into any of the other parts of speech like nouns, verbs, or prepositions) that most other languages do not have and that express this "both-and" paradoxical doubleness. They are *men* and *de*, which mean "on the one hand" and "on the other hand". These two particles are used very frequently in both Greek philosophy and the New Testament because they express the very frequent thought pattern of a both-and paradox. On the one hand, God; on the other hand, man. On the one hand, good; on the other hand, evil. On the one hand, death, on the other hand, life and resurrection. On the one hand, destiny, on the other hand, choice. On the one hand, loss, on the other hand, gain.

The primary paradox in Mary—both in her words and in her life and her actual being—is the paradox of grace and nature, especially God and Man, which are reconciled in the Incarnation, i.e., the baby in her very body. On the one hand, she ascribes all that is in her to divine grace: "he who is mighty has done great things for me, / and holy is his name" (Lk 1:49). She magnifies not herself, but the Lord

(Lk 1:46, the very first and thematic line of her Magnificat). Yet, on the other hand, she also affirms her own greatness in her very littleness and truly prophesies that "all generations will call me blessed" (Lk 1:48). She is raised the highest because she lowers herself to be the humblest—like Christ. "[M]any that are first will be last, and the last first" (Mt 19:30; 20:16; Mk 9:35).

This is, in fact, the primary Christian paradox, both (1) objectively or theologically, concerning nature and grace, the natural and the supernatural, and also (2) subjectively or psychologically, concerning the death of self-will and the fulfillment of self-will. (1) The angel calls her "full of grace", and this is itself a paradox because "grace" is not nature, yet it becomes her nature to the fullest. It is a paradox because nature is not grace, yet in her human nature becomes absolutely "full of grace" (Lk 1:28). (2) Her affirmation of this theological paradox becomes her psychological paradox: that the more nature (human nature) denies its mastery of itself, the more it becomes master of itself. The more it denies its own self-will and its own autonomy, the more its deepest will and search for happiness is fulfilled. The more I let God's will, not mine, be done, the more my will is done. The more I empty myself and open myself to grace, the more full I become. The more I die to myself, the more I live. The more I give myself away, the more I find myself. The more "down" I bow, the taller I rise.

God designed this paradox in human nature. The self is given to us for this ultimate purpose: to give itself away, not to get, and thus to find the only way to get. Life is given to us to die to and thus to find the only way to life, through death and resurrection; to become itself by denying itself daily in *agape* love and by totally forgetting itself in mystical experience. This is the paradoxical wisdom of all true religion, and Mary exemplifies it perfectly on the human level because her Son reveals this paradox perfectly on the divine level. If even God lowers Himself to become our slave (Phil 2:5–11) and dies for us as our sacrificial Lamb, then our own supreme destiny and joy must also be to "let this mind be in you, which was also in Christ Jesus" (Phil 2:5 KJV). That is the secret of Mary's paradoxical logic.

For Christ revealed two things, the two most important things for us to know, and they are both paradoxes. He revealed most perfectly not only who God is but also who we are, since he is perfect man as well as perfect God. Both are paradoxical. On the divine side, Christ revealed who God is most clearly when He showed the depths of God's love for us by dying for us, i.e., by doing the last thing Eternal Life Itself apparently could ever possibly do. And on the human side, Christ was the most creative and original man in history precisely because He was history's greatest conformist to God the Father. He both shows us and tells us that we are ourselves only when, like Him, we do not try to "be ourselves". That *kenosis*, or self-emptying (Phil 2:7) is His (and Mary's) answer to the most important of all questions: What is the meaning of life, what is our life's ultimate good and end and purpose and fulfillment—and therefore the secret of joy? Ask any saint. In no saint is this clearer and simpler than in Mary.

Of course this is not just logic, this is religion. But the logic of paradox is its form. Every religion in the world knows something of this paradox. Although the religions of the world differ radically about theology, about God or the gods, they do not disagree as radically about man and the meaning of human life: it is to get yourself off the throne of your life, to overcome egotism with altruism. Buddhist atheists and Christian theists, Confucian legalists and Taoist romantics, Jewish humanists and Hindu pantheists, Sufi mystics and Sunni legalists all say this, in different degrees and in different ways. All the sages teach it; Christ alone perfectly incarnates it.

~

Philosophically speaking, the structure of this paradoxical thinking could be called Hegelian, for Hegel made famous the "dialectic" (logical structure) of "thesis-antithesis-higher synthesis" in which the apparent contradiction between one idea or reality (the "thesis") and its opposite (the "anti-thesis") is overcome and reconciled by a higher, more profound and inclusive point of view, the "higher synthesis". Stripped of its questionable Hegelian content, this Hegelian logic of "dialectic" has proved very useful even to some of Hegel's strongest critics, notably Marx and Kierkegaard. Marx changed the content of the dialectic from Hegel's spiritualist monism or pantheism to a materialist monism (both of which are radical errors) and applied it to economic and political history, the "higher synthesis" of past feudalism and present capitalism being the future communist Utopia (which of course brought deep happiness and peace to the hundreds of millions who were murdered by it). Kierkegaard changed the content from Hegelian collectivism, pantheism, and rationalism to individualism, theism, and fideism and applied it to the three "stages on life's way", (1) the "aesthetic" or sensory-worldly-egotistic, (2) the "ethical", and (3) the "religious", which overcomes the conflict between personal egotism (stage 1) and impersonal duty (stage 2) and which reconciles or synthesizes the individuality, concreteness, and fascination of the "aesthetic" with the altruism, principledness, and responsibility of the "ethical".

~

Mary is a both-and thinker. Our usual dualisms, double-nesses, separations, or divorces in thought are united and reconciled in her: natural and supernatural, masculine and feminine, body and soul, optimism and pessimism, joy and pain. Women are better than men at unifying, relating, or reconciling opposite things, whether these things are ideas, emotions, or people. They also reconcile ideas and thoughts with emotions better than men do, for there are more connectors between the two hemispheres of their brains than between those of men—between the hemisphere that thinks and speaks and the one that feels. That is why women tend to speak *more* when they feel most deeply, while men tend to speak *less*.

It is a great oversimplification, and it is so "politically incorrect", that you will be fired from the presidency of Harvard if you even suggest that it deserves discussion (see the next paragraph), but it is true: men and women are different. The difference is not total or absolute, but it is real. It is not quantitative (literally "all" men or "all" women) but it is qualitative: a difference in *nature*. Men make wars; women make peace. Little girls play with dollhouses; little boys knock them over with trucks. This difference is in thought as well as in action. Men analyze; women synthesize. Men contrast; women connect. Men calculate; women intuit. Women see the "big picture"; men break it into parts and steps, which is an essential feature of the scientific method. Most successful couples counselors are women. Men become theorists; women become poets. Men are

mathmakers; women are mythmakers. These are not stereotypes that are socially constructed and, therefore, socially
deconstructible. They are not man-made stereotypes but divinely designed archetypes. Shocking as it sounds, we did
not invent our own sexuality. God did. And what God has
split asunder, let man not try to join together and confuse.
Lincoln said: "If you call a tail a leg, how many legs does
a dog have? The answer is four: calling a tail a leg doesn't
make it a leg." If a man calls himself a woman, how many
ovaries does she have? None: calling a man a woman does
not make him a woman.

This is simply factual and commonsensical, but it is "hurt-
ful" "hate speech" today and generates the defense of "trig-
ger warnings" and "safe spaces" like Ivy League universities,
where such blasphemies may not be heard. Islamic soci-
eties are not the only ones that censor any whiff of blasphemy against the ruling religion. But this "blasphemy" is
evidence-based fact. There are no fewer than fifty-one phys-
iological differences between the male and female brain. And
this explains empirical facts such as why women freely tend
to gravitate to the humanities and the "soft sciences" while
men tend to gravitate to the "hard sciences". Yet these facts
are forbidden facts. Ask Larry Summers. He was the popular president of "liberal" Harvard but was fired for daring
to suggest, in a faculty meeting, that Harvard might attract
more women to the hard sciences by discussing possible reasons why Harvard had failed to do so, including the idea, accepted by all cultures in history except our own, that perhaps
there were some innate differences between the psyches of
males and females. Summers did not believe or recommend
the idea, but he was fired for recommending that it even be
allowed to be discussed. Today's "soft totalitarianism" (to
use De Tocqueville's term) uses fear instead of force to sup-

press all dissent. Heretics are still hunted down and excommunicated today, but not by the Church. In fact, Catholics are not the perpetrators but the victims of the Inquisition today. The roles have been exactly reversed.

There is a divinely ordained biological image of the spiritual paradox of fullness by emptiness that can be found in human nature. It is called sex. The distinctive organ in a woman is an emptiness: a womb. The distinctive organ in a man is an addition: a penis. Yet, paradoxically, this means that a woman can be full in a way a man cannot: full of a second life, a baby. Freud thought women had "penis envy"; it is at least equally likely that men have "womb envy", or at least awe toward this uniquely female power to bring forth new life from within rather than merely to cause it from without, like making a deposit in the bank and then watching it accumulate interest. The saints and mystics often say that to God every human soul is feminine, a spiritual womb waiting to be impregnated by divine life (but, of course, God is a gentleman and awaits our permission, so many remain barren). Surrender (the literal meaning of *islam*) is an erotic necessity biologically, psychologically, and religiously. It is the secret of joy on all three levels.

This analogy between religion and sex is obviously closely connected with the refusal of religious Jews, Christians, and Muslims to call God "She", only "He". This is often denounced as male chauvinism, but it is closer to female chauvinism, since we are all feminine to God. And thus we are living paradoxes: filled only by being empty, active only by being receptive. Those "feminists" who protest against this blatantly obvious connection between the sexuality of our bodies and that of our souls always tend to Gnosticism, spiritualism, or dualism; that is, they separate the soul from the body, spirituality from sexuality. For once the psycho-somatic unity is accepted, the innate sexuality of the soul naturally follows from the innate sexuality of the body.

Much of modern "feminism" is a flight from everything feminine—like the Amazons, who cut off their own breasts ("A-mazon" means literally "without a breast") the better to imitate men in shooting arrows without impediment. If that is a feminism, then cannibalism is a humanism. It is a perfect example of what Hitler, with the wisdom of the serpent, advocated as the "Big Lie", like calling a Communist dictatorship "the people's republic".

⁓

We seem to have strayed far from logic, but only because we think of the logic of textbooks and abstract rules rather than the logic of real bodies and souls.

The ontological center of the psychological paradox that we have been exploring is the Incarnation. Mary is literally at the center and heart of this paradox of "the God-man synthesis". The "impossible" marriage of the divine and the human is celebrated in her body, the new Garden of Eden.

Paradoxes, mysteries, and miracles do not contradict logic because they do not contradict truth. Only falsehood contradicts truth; truth never does. But the form truth takes is often paradoxical, mysterious, or miraculous. Paradoxes are not illogical because they are only apparent contradictions, based on an analogy between two different meanings of a term. And mysteries do not contradict logic; they only contradict our claim to understand them fully.

Faith contradicts reason only when it is false, never when it is true, since truth never contradicts truth. And "all truth is God's truth", whether made known by supernatural revelation or by natural reason. This divine Teacher wrote two textbooks, nature and Scripture, and they never contradict each other because He does not contradict Himself. The two books are not only noncontradictory, but they are intimately related and interdependent, for, on the one hand, we must begin by faith (trust) in reason as our instrument because reason cannot prove itself, any more than light can illumine itself; and, on the other hand, we cannot begin by faith unless reason understands it: you have to know how to read before you can read the Bible. You have to believe in thought before you can think, and you have to think what you believe before you can believe it.

You did not expect all that in a chapter on logic, did you?

Chapter IV

MARY'S METAPHYSICS

I begin with a chain of three surprising but valid syllogisms.

(1) MAJOR PREMISE: Metaphysics is defined by Aristotle and Aquinas as "the knowledge of first causes".

MINOR PREMISE: Christ is in truth the first cause of all creation, for God created the universe only by "speaking" His "Word". Since Christ is "the Word of God", Genesis 1 is all about Christ.

CONCLUSION: Therefore, metaphysics is the knowledge of Christ.

(2) MAJOR PREMISE: Metaphysics is the knowledge of Christ.

MINOR PREMISE: Christ is a (Divine) Person.

CONCLUSION: Therefore metaphysics is the knowledge of a (Divine) Person.

(3) MAJOR PREMISE: Metaphysics is the knowledge of a (Divine) Person.

MINOR PREMISE: When it comes to knowing a person, whether human or divine, love is the highest and deepest knowledge.

CONCLUSION: Therefore, the love of the Divine Person who is Christ is metaphysics at its highest and deepest. In other words, whoever loves and therefore knows Christ best is the greatest metaphysician.

Is there any doubt about her name?

The Three Divisions of Metaphysics

Metaphysics deals with two basic sets of questions, which are sometimes called the questions of "general metaphysics" and of "special metaphysics". General metaphysics asks: What is being *qua* being, being itself, or being universally? Special metaphysics asks two more specific questions, since there are two specifically different kinds of being, eternal and temporal, infinite and finite, Creator and creature. Theology asks about the first, cosmology about the second. Thus we have three chapters about metaphysics as we had three chapters about epistemology (methodology [chap. 1], epistemology [chap. 2], and logic [chap. 3]), namely, (4) metaphysics, (5) theology, and (6) cosmology.

There is a near identity between general metaphysics and theology because at the summit of Being Itself we find the Supreme Being, the Prime Being; and, therefore, at the summit of general metaphysics we find the metaphysics of God, Who is Being Itself in person. His self-revealed eternal and essential name is "I AM", the unity of person and being, "I-ness" and "am-ness". (See Father Norris Clarke's profound little book *Person and Being*.) To know best what Being itself is, we must know God.

Mary is the best of all metaphysicians for that reason: because no merely human being ever knew (or knows or ever will know) God more perfectly than Mary. For she lives the perfect and complete human relationship to all three Divine Persons: she is the perfect daughter to the Father, the perfect mother to the Son, and the perfect spouse to the Holy Spirit. And since God is the ultimate answer to the metaphysical question, it follows that Mary's metaphysics is the ultimate metaphysics and the standard of perfection for metaphysical wisdom.

Of course, we must make two qualifications and distinctions.

First, Mary's metaphysics is "special metaphysics", not "general metaphysics". It is a deep knowledge of the First Being, not about being-as-such or being-in-general. Yet there are profound implications about being-in-general embedded in her knowledge of the First Being, as we shall see.

Second, Mary's mode of knowing is *kennen* rather than *wissen*, or *connaître* rather than *savoir*, or "personal knowledge" rather than "impersonal knowledge". It is not a "science" of metaphysics, even in the older, broader meaning of "science" according to which philosophy is also a science.

That does not make her knowledge inferior to the knowledge in which philosophers specialize. Just the opposite: it makes it superior. Her knowledge of God, the true God, the First Cause and Prime Being, came through two channels: (1) through the infallible divine revelation God gave to His chosen people, the Jews, through their history and tradition and through their Scriptures (and if you are allergic to infallibility, you are allergic to God) and (2) through her uniquely innocent and perfect personal experience and prayer. Both of these channels of knowledge are matters of personal faith, or trust, rather than impersonal, detached "reason" and "science". But that knowledge has revolutionary implications for the impersonal questions of metaphysics.

Of course, Mary does not address any of the abstract questions of general metaphysics as a science of universal being, or being as such, questions like the correct concepts of the relation between the One and the Many, or Cause and Effect, or Essence and Existence. In that sense, she is no more a metaphysician than a physician. She is not a college philosophy professor! Yet even in the abstract or general dimension of metaphysics, we can see truths that are implied both in her personal experience and in her Jewish tradition, which she brought to perfection like the point of an arrow entering a holy target. Those general implications are what this chapter is about. The next one is about theology more specifically, or "special metaphysics". The two enterprises overlap, run into each other, and imply each other most intimately, and so do these two chapters.

Just as there is a natural overlap between the answers to the two questions of metaphysics—the question of being and the question of the Prime Being—so there is also a natural overlap between the theoretical and the practical questions, both about being as such and about the Prime Being. But though their answers greatly overlap, the questions themselves can be distinguished into three groups: questions about being as such (metaphysics), questions about the Prime Being in Himself (theology), and questions about our personal relationship to the Prime Being (religion). So we have three distinct chapters (3, 4, and 14), even though these three overlap like the three circles of a Venn diagram.

Two Questions within General Metaphysics: Analogy and Hierarchy

You will probably have to read the following section much more slowly and carefully and repeatedly than most of the other stuff in this book. It is supremely abstract.

Two of the issues in general metaphysics are:

(1) whether being is univocal (that is, one and the same in meaning in all of its instances) or analogical (that is, having partly the same and partly different meanings in its different instances); and

(2) whether being is hierarchical, a "more or less", like steps on a ladder, or whether it is simple and egalitarian, without degrees of inequality.

The two issues are related, though not identical; for if being is hierarchical, and if the differences between the higher and lower parts of the hierarchy of being are differences in kind or quality rather than merely in degree or quantity, that means it must be analogical rather than univocal. However, the converse does not necessarily follow. It is logically possible for being to be analogical in meaning in some other way than by its real instances being hierarchical. If you did not understand that technical and abstract philosophical point, all I can say is: welcome to the normal 99 percent of the human race.

The order of our two chapters on metaphysics is logical rather than experiential. Mary comes at the questions of metaphysics inductively rather than deductively; that is, she derives her (implicit) knowledge of general metaphysics from her knowledge of special metaphysics (knowledge of God, theology) rather than vice versa. In contrast to this, it is natural for philosophers and theologians to begin with general metaphysics and then apply these general principles deductively to special metaphysics, or the metaphysics of God. Mary does the opposite. Insofar as there are any general universal metaphysical principles in her, she gets them from God in particular. She goes from the concrete to the abstract.

(By the way, "concrete" does not mean "material". "Concrete" means "individual", and "abstract" means "universal". Saint Michael the Archangel is concrete, while "cement" is abstract. My act of thinking about matter is concrete, while "matter" is abstract. Universals ["essences", "quiddities", "whats"] are abstract, whether they are physical or spiritual; individual instances are concrete, whether they are physical or spiritual.)

Mary's Jewish theism does not allow Being to be univocal (one and the same essential meaning in all instances). The doctrine that God creates makes "being" analogical, for God IS Being, while creatures only HAVE it, on loan, so to speak. All other beings were created *ex nihilo* (from nothing). For the being of the Creator is eternal and necessary and in need of no cause. It is independent of any other being. But the being of every creature (created being) is temporal (even angels have spiritual time) and has a beginning and is contingent, i.e., dependent on its cause. God IS being by His eternal essence, while everything else only HAS being, for its essence is not existence. It does not have to exist. Everything except God is a might-not-have-been. You cannot give what you do not have, and only God the Creator has being (existence) by His own eternal and necessary nature or essence, while creatures GET being from His gift of creating. We only borrow, in time, what God eternally has and is, namely, being or existence.

Being (existence) is God's essence, but it is not the essence of any creature. So if we ask the great question that was formulated by Hegel and made famous by Heidegger, the question that he called "the fundamental question of metaphysics", namely, "Why does anything at all exist rather than nothing?", the answer is not the same when that "anything" refers to God and when it refers to creatures. The two kinds of being exist for different reasons: God from inside, so to speak, and creatures from outside. God exists because God is God—He IS existence. But creatures GET existence. They exist only because God creates them. Thus, both God and creatures exist because of God.

So the child's question "But if God created everything else, who created God?" is really a misunderstanding of the word "God". It literally means "Who made the being that nobody made?" or "Who created the Uncreated Creator?" It is like the question "What positive number precedes the very first positive number?"

Since God is Being Itself and everything else only borrows being, "being" is analogical, not univocal. And since independent and eternal being is being in a higher sense than dependent and temporal being, "being" is hierarchical, not egalitarian. The universe is not a democracy, however politically incorrect it may be to admit that. God did not ask His creatures to vote either Himself or themselves into existence.

~

All this is implied in Jewish theism or creationism and is not specific to Mary only. It *is* specific to Judaism. No other ancient language had a word for creation out of nothing (*bara'*) because no other culture had any concept of it.

So the question arises: Does Mary herself say anything explicitly metaphysical?

There is a very strong answer to that question: Yes! The most important word she ever spoke is the most metaphysical word there is. It is the word *fiat* (in Latin translation), which means "let it be!" or simply "Be!" (It is a command.) It is like the word "Amen", or the word "Yes". It is the word God spoke in creating the universe. And Mary now speaks it again, not to creation but to incarnation; to God's offer, through His angel, to make of Mary something apparently unthinkable: the Mother of God.

In speaking her word, Mary gives God a blank check.

And she signs this check with her name. In Jewish culture, your name is not a label, it is a destiny, and it is your divinely designed identity. That is why no Orthodox Jew may change his name. Only God can change your identity and your destiny, so only God may change your name, as God did to Abram ("Abraham"), to Sarai ("Sarah"), and to Jacob ("Israel"), and as Jesus did to Simon ("Peter").

To agree with God and to echo His command of "Be!" is easy for us to do with respect to most creatures. It is easy to affirm the existence of angels, stars, water, air, fruits, flowers, puppy dogs, and pussycats. It is harder to say that "Yes" to hurricanes and hemorrhoids and hyenas. It is even harder to say it to the sufferings and diseases that God's Providence deliberately allows to enter our lives and the lives of those we love, especially when we cannot understand them. This was Mary's heroic task, especially regarding the sufferings of her Son. Of course, she did not foresee them at the Annunciation, but in giving God a blank check, she allowed them.

She loved Christ and, therefore, "identified with" Him (for loving another gives you another identity without taking away your own identity) and embraced all of His sufferings more than any other creature did. In *The Passion of the Christ*, we see her accompanying Christ at every step on the *via dolorosa*, the dolorous way of the Cross, as He clutches His Cross like a teddy bear with his bleeding, torn, exhausted body. She asks Him: "Why do you have to do all this? I do not understand." He could have redeemed the world with one drop of His Precious Blood; why does He have to enter into maximum torture? It is incredibly hard, it is almost impossible, for her to say "Be!" to that.

His answer is the greatest line in cinematic history: "See, Mother, I make all things new."

When Mary says her *fiat*, or "Yes", to God, she says it to, and by grace participates in, God's act of creation by which He said the very same word to the whole universe in creating it: not only its present but also its future, including the suffering of His Son and all the human cells in His Body. "Let there be light" included "Let there be the buzzing of Beelzebub's flies around the Blood on the Cross." Like Him, she says "Be!" to all this. She affirms being—all being. For in some mysterious way (not the way of pantheism, but of creationism), all being is God's being, as all goodness is His goodness and all truth is His truth and all beauty is His beauty. God willed it all into existence, either directly (the good) or indirectly (the evil that He turned to a greater good).

The difference between God's perfect divine will and Mary's perfect human will is that Mary (and all the saints in imitation of her, and all of us in imitation of all the saints) says "Be!" or *fiat* to that which precedes her, namely, God and His will and His plan and His creation and His mysterious Providence; while God says "Be!" to that which follows and obeys Him, namely, the whole creation. Even those who disobey Him obey His will, His plan. Mary says Yes to God's whole will, including His will to permit the greatest moral evil in history, the murder of His Son—and hers.

In both cases, God's creative will and Mary's instrumental will, the word *fiat* is creative; it brings about new being, in two different ways: God makes being be, and Mary lets being be. When He sends His Son to her, He sends His Son's whole life, including His Passion and death; and when Mary freely receives Him, she receives His whole life, including His Passion and death. All three Persons of the Trinity always work together, so all three were acting when

God used the moral non-being or anti-being of sin (Judas, Pilate, Herod, Caiaphas, Rome) and the physical non-being of Christ's suffering and death to conquer and destroy both sin and death; and Mary was His freely consenting instrument. Her *fiat* to that was the profoundest metaphysical statement any human being in history ever made.

Creative Receptivity

A word is also a will, for words do not just happen but are said, i.e., willed. This is true of our words and of God's.

Both God and Mary speak the creative word *fiat*, which is the command to "be" or "let it be."

Both God's purely active word (and will) and Mary's receptive word (and will) are creative. God's creativity is initiative, like a man's act of impregnating a woman. Mary's creativity is receptive, like a woman's act of accepting a man. It is not passive; it is receptive. Created nature is passive to God the Father as well as finite and temporal; but the Word of God, who is the Son of God, is receptive to the Father actively, infinitely, and eternally.

Since Mary accepts God's act of creativity totally, with no restrictions, and since God's act of creativity is responsible for all of unfree nature and free human history, therefore Mary's *fiat* is her "yes" not only to God but also to all of nature and history. God is the middle term between Mary and all of nature and history. Mary says "Let it be!" to God, and God says "Be!" to all of nature and history; therefore, Mary says "Let it be!" to all of nature and history as well as to her role as the Mother of the Redeemer. For the Redeemer is also the Creator.

Both God's act of saying (and willing) "Be" and Mary's

act of saying (and willing) "let it be!" to that will are free acts. In that one word, Mary literally co-operated, "operated with", or "worked with" God's will as an active, free, creative instrumental cause. Her conformity is not passivity because it is con-formity to the form that is purely active, namely, God's will. God is not passive, and insofar as we actively align our will with Him, we also are not passive, even when we are receptive and even when we simply say "Thy will be done." That is not passive resignation, much less defeatism or despair.

This understanding of Mary's *fiat* implies that receptivity is not passivity and is not metaphysically inferior to activity, for both activity and receptivity are creative. And this is a metaphysical revolution that Aristotle and even Aquinas did not quite reach. The next paragraph explains why.

Aristotle and Aquinas both say (rightly) that perfection of being is *actuality* rather than potentiality or potency. And Aquinas then goes on to apply this to *activity*, which is not quite the same as *actuality*, since he (rightly) distinguishes actuality, or actual existence, which he calls "first act", from activity, or action, which he calls "second act". "Second act" always "follows from" "first act" or (to put the same point backwards), "first act" always "flows over into" "second act". Even a rock acts on the earth by making a rut and on other bodies by gravity and on your journey when it blocks your road.

The more real a thing is, the more active it is. For example, ideas are not real beings at all but only mental beings. They are only potentially real beings because they do not act on any real things but are passive copies of things, like images in a mirror.

The revolutionary addition to this Thomistic metaphysics is that receptivity (active receptivity, anyway, like a woman's role in sexual intercourse) can be as active and creative, and thus as actual, as metaphysically real, as activity. This is not true of purely passive receptivity, which is matter's relation to form, e.g., space's relation to being divided into the within and the without by a border, such as a box. (If you did not understand that point, "dinna fash yourself", as the Scots say, or, in New York language, "fagettaboutit.")

This principle of active and creative receptivity is based on and begins in the Trinity. For the Son *receives* everything from the Father. He is eternally "begotten" (but not "created") by the Father (Jn 3:16). His mind receives and passes on the Father's mind (Jn 7:16). His will conforms to the Father's will (Jn 5:30). Yet He is equal to the Father (Jn 10:30; Col 1:19), equally divine, perfect, eternal, and actual.

Since everything in creation follows from and resembles the Creator (it has no other place to go to get any kind of its being!), this principle manifests itself also in nature, or the creation. Lao Tzu profoundly perceived this in the *Tao Te Ching*, when he taught that the "way" ("Tao") of the wise gets its power from its conformity to the "way" of nature, which in turn gets its power from its conformity to the eternal, unknowable, absolute "Way", from Its self-giving, self-emptying, and receptivity. His favorite images of this power of receptivity are water, willows, women, windows, and wombs. Thus the wise empty themselves of egotism and serve (like Christ!) rather than assert their egos and dominate and conquer, like Sauron in *The Lord of the Rings* or like technology, which Francis Bacon defined as "man's conquest of nature". Christ is not God's spiritual technology. That is why He is reluctant to "fix" problems by power, by miracles. Sauron plays God, but Sauron is not God because God is not Sauron. God is love.

This principle about receptivity also manifests itself in human sex and procreation, which is the favorite image of the mystics. God is our (spiritual) Husband (Is 54:5), not our Wife. We do not impregnate Him; He impregnates us. Our supreme power is our receptivity to Him and His life.

The principle also manifests itself in ethics, in what Marcel calls "creative fidelity"; in the fact that our conformity and obedience to the moral law and our responding to others' needs are not in any way weaknesses or imperfections but perfections of our being. And this moral principle is also an ontological one, for the principles of metaphysics, being universal, must apply also to ethics. In fact, the more moral we are, the more real we are. Moral goodness increases our happiness only because it increases our being. Saints are more real, more fully real, more alive than sinners. Heaven is more solid than earth; Hell is full of ghosts. (It is all in C. S. Lewis' *The Great Divorce*.)

This is why Mary does not need to speak many words or perform many actions in Scripture. She is the archetype of the woman. Men need to speak loudly, or at least, if they speak softly, to carry a big stick. They need to make themselves something by doing things. Their identity, like their sex organ, points outward to the world. Women's identity is inside, like their sex organs. Their being is more important than their doing.

In social ethics, this principle manifests itself in a revolutionary way, raising the value of all natural "receptivities" and "conformities" and "obediences": of wives to husbands, citizens to rulers, servants to masters, and children to parents. In each case, the receivers and "conformers" are not inferior to the actors, doers, and givers. As the Son perfectly obeys His Father, with both His mind (teaching) and His will (actions), without thereby manifesting any inferiority of being or value, so these four perennial human relationships are transformed into something that fits neither the ancient relationship of lordship, superiority, and hierarchy without equality nor the modern relationship of equality without lordship or hierarchy.

For metaphysical principles are pregnant with consequences. They are like women who have many children. (Children are certainly "consequences" of sexual intercourse, however much we see them as "accidents"!)

That last very obvious point, in parentheses and its denial in our contraceptive culture, makes the following short tangent a temptation I cannot resist. Our modern sex education courses have as their primary effect an astonishing ignorance or deliberate denial of that fact, the single most important and most obvious fact (and value) about the whole subject about which this new "education" claims to "educate". The word "education" comes from the Latin *e-ducare*, which means "to lead out". The thought is that education leads the student out of the cave of darkness and ignorance. In the case of modern sex education, its meaning has become exactly reversed: a leading out from light and truth into darkness and denial. This is part of the modern "Enlightenment", which is really "the Endarkenment" or (as Buber calls it) "the Eclipse of God".

Once again Hitler has been proved right about mankind's gullibility to the "Big Lie". The bigger the lie, the more we fall for it. The fatter the worm on the Devil's hook, the more we poor fish bite it. It is still, as the Psalmist said millennia ago, only the fool who says in his heart that "there is no God" in the sexual act, or, in the words of modern "feminists" (another Big Lie), "keep your rosaries off our ovaries." "Get out, God", is unfortunately sacramental: it effects what it signifies, for God is a gentleman and obeys our deepest will both when we obey His will and when we do not. Or, as Lewis says, "There are only two kinds of people in the end: those who say to God, 'Thy will be done,' and those to whom God says, in the end, 'Thy will be done.'"

Mary exemplifies all these principles. In fact, instead of saying that Mary is like metaphysics in this way, perhaps we should say that metaphysics is like Mary. Especially concerning her pregnancy. Its "consequence", the Being to whom she gave birth, is the total opposite of an "accident". He is "our life, our sweetness, and our hope". And that is the whole reason why she is, too.

The Metaphysics of "I AM"

Mary did not figure out who or what God is. She was taught it, in her Jewish tradition, which was handed down, not from man, but from God. God Himself gave the answer to the question "Who are you?" to Moses, the greatest prophet (Dt 34:10), from the burning bush. In Judaism, your name is your identity, and God's name is not any finite and definable being, like Zeus or Jupiter, but unlimited Being itself: not "I am this" or "I am that", but simply "I AM", and "I AM WHO I AM."

Mary did not understand the meaning of that infinitely and incomparably profound word in the way that most philosophers do, e.g., as "the being whose essence is existence", or as "eternal and necessary being"; but she did understand those two words. (In Hebrew, they are just one word, "JHWH", the word so sacred no Jew dares ever utter it or write it.) "I" means "person", and "am" means "being" or "existence".

Of course, Mary did not understand philosophically *how* those two—being and person, the "am" and the "I"—could be one; but she *did* understand *that* they were one in God, simply because God said so in giving us His own eternal, essential name. She knew it by faith, of course, by listening to God through Moses and to Moses through her rabbis and by reading her Scriptures. She did not know it by taking philosophy courses or by reading philosophy books. If that is the only way we can understand what is, we are in desperately deep doo-doo.

But if she had heard Saint Thomas Aquinas explain it in nontechnical language, I think she would have understood intuitively and immediately.

What God said to Moses was like a seed, a germ, an embryo planted in our minds; and Saint Thomas worked out some but not all of its implications. The implication we are now exploring, the ultimate oneness of person and being, was left to modern man to explicate and formulate, because modern man, whatever his errors and shortcomings, is more self-conscious and psychological and more explicitly aware of "personhood" or "personality". But what Aquinas did say was the foundation of this metaphysical revolution. He said, in *Summa Theologica* I, 29, 3, that "Person designates the highest being in nature."

This means not merely that persons have more powers and more virtues (and more vices) than things below us on the great chain of being, but that persons are the highest beings *in their being*; that persons are the most real beings, the beings that are the most full of being. As Mary was "full of grace", persons are "full of being". What being is by its own fullness and excellence, as distinct from anything added to it, is personhood; everything less than person is less than the fullness of being, like a statue with some chips chipped out of it or like an ocean that is bounded by a shore. Being of itself is unbounded. And so is person. Even old Aristotle said that "the human soul is, in a way, all things." He did not mean pantheism; he meant that by being able to know any and all beings, our mind is potentially infinite. It is not actually infinite; only God is that. But it is like the number series: for every finite number, there can always be a greater, a more; there is no highest number. There is no limit to the number of finite things that the human mind can know, that the human will can choose, and that the human heart can love. Goodness, truth, and beauty are three "transcendental" properties of all being and of God.

To have a mind and a will and a heart is what it means to be a person. So from this abstract universal principle that persons have the most being, it follows that God, the supreme being, the standard for the being of beings, the supreme degree of reality, must be a Person (or Persons), must be "I" (or "We"); that being in its purity and fullness is not an "it is" but an "I AM." Everything less than a person is less in being than a person.

We miss this because we think of being, or existence, as a fact rather than an act. To say that God is unlimited existence sounds like reducing God to an abstraction; but existence is not an abstraction. In fact, it is a verb (*esse*, "to be" in Latin) rather than a noun. It means the act of exist*ing*. (As before, if you just don't get that, welcome to the rest of the human race. I just barely get it myself.)

Another corollary, which Mary also knew without articulating the metaphysical principle which grounds it, is that since we, too, though contingent and finite and temporal, are persons, that is, "I's", two things logically follow: that God must have created us, since we are contingent and finite and temporal; and that He created us in His own image,

Mary's Philosophy

since we are persons, too. So we, too, in a created and contingent (dependent) and temporal way, have the highest kind of being. The consequences of this metaphysics echo everywhere, in anthropology as well as in theology. It does not lower Being, but it raises Person.

Let's summarize the unique principles of this metaphysics of the burning bush.

1. God is not just "a" being, even "the" highest being, but Being Itself: "I AM WHO I AM."
2. God is also Person, "I".
3. God is the unity of Person and Being, of "I" and "AM".
4. Therefore, the standard and "prime analogate" for being is personhood. To be fully real is to be a person.

This justifies calling Mary a metaphysician. For in knowing God as Person, she knew Being Itself.

If this seems a "stretch", I refer the reader to the astonishing yet upon examination eminently reasonable assertion of Gabriel Marcel, a philosopher not given to exaggeration or sentimentality, that "the study of sanctity . . . is the true ontology [metaphysics]." This startling conclusion follows from two premises: that saints are the standard for personhood, because they actualize and thus reveal the meaning of human personhood better than any others, and that personhood is the standard for being, as explained above.

I predict that future theistic philosophers will be more surprised that no one before Marcel articulated this principle than they will be surprised by the principle itself. They will be surprised, not at the principle, but at the fact that we are surprised by it.

The Metaphysical Imperative

Behind and below and beyond the reason's intellectual imperative (the demand for truth, the honest love of truth) and the will's moral imperative (the demand for goodness) and the heart's affective imperative (the demand for beauty and lovability), there is a metaphysical imperative, an ontological demand, a thirst for being. Mircea Eliade, who knows the primitive or prehistoric mind better than almost anyone (see his *The Sacred and the Profane*), speaks of this ontological thirst or demand for being as the motive behind all the myths and practices of primitive mankind, as a kind of unconscious bagpipe drone or organ point or pedal point to all future human cultural "music". That is what is behind all the gods, goods, and goals, all the demands, desires, and dreams, all the loves, longings, and legends, of all human cultures. It comes, not just from the mind or the will or the feelings, but from the "heart", in the sense of the deepest, most mysterious center of the "I", and the deepest heart of all three of those powers.

The demand is not to BE Being itself, to become God (except in Shankara's Hinduism), but to attain it, to unite with it, or at least to approach it, to conform to it, to be like it—both intellectually (to know the truth) and volitionally (to do the right thing) and affectively (to be rightly moved, to love the love-worthy and hate the hate-worthy). (God is an "It" for Shankara and jnana yoga, a "Him" for Ramanuja and bhakti yoga, and a "them" for popular practical polytheistic Hinduism.)

This ontological imperative expresses itself spontaneously and naturally when we pray, when our bodies (which are less alienated from Being than our souls are) teach our souls to (1) be silent (since Being is first and therefore speaks first, before we speak back); and (2) to kneel (for Being acts and comes to us first before we walk to it); and (3) to bow (for Being conquers us and we surrender and fall down like a pussycat, Beta to Alpha); and (4) to fold our hands (for Being touches us before we can reach out and touch it and because we are now no longer armed and acting but trustingly defenseless and receiving); and (5) to shut our eyes—for Being knows us before we can know it—for if it is a Person, it is the subject, the Knower, the "I AM", while we are the known object; and even if it is not a Person, in any case, it is too bright for us to see: "No man can see God's face and live" unless his name is either Moses or Job.

We naturally do all this when approaching God in prayer even when we do not understand it. This right relationship to God is the essence of prayer. And it is also the essence of life insofar as we can conform our lives to prayer, i.e., to metaphysical truth, that is, insofar as we let our lives be judged by Being rather than judging it, as arrogantly rationalistic so-called philosophers often do. (They are really Sophists, not philosophers.)

Mary is the perfect non-Sophist.

This ontological thirst is the ultimate motive for prayer and for all action and work that emerge from prayer and conform to its vision. This is the heart of the saint and the sage, and Mary is the most perfect one. She best lives the supreme wisdom of Saint Catherine's vision, when God summarized the truth that is both the foundation and the beginning of all human wisdom and also its end or summit in two points: "I'm God, you're not."

Our bodies bow because our souls command them to bow and kneel and be silent and fold hands and shut eyes. But our bodies also command and condition our souls to do all these things. Saint Francis called his body "Brother Ass". That is exactly right. A donkey is a humble and useful beast. That is why Christ rode one into Jerusalem. Bodies are far more obedient and wise than souls, as Augustine discovered, to his amazement, in book 7 of his *Confessions*, when he discovered that our bodies obey our souls far better than our souls (minds and wills) obey themselves, far better than they obey their own commands. Souls disobey their own deepest desires; bodies do not. Souls are divided from themselves (read Romans 7:15–25), bodies are not, as long as they are still alive.

Whatever we can learn from all the saints, we can learn best of all from the greatest saint. We can learn about her from them—they cast new light on her—and we can also learn about them from her—she casts the clearest light on them. We can learn about sunlight from studying moonlight, and we can learn about moonlight from studying sunlight. Mary is distinctive only in quantity, not quality. It is the same quality (innocence, wisdom, light), not a unique and arcane and unknowable one. The more we look at Mary's uniqueness, the more we see that she is not unique but universal. Like Being.

Chapter V

MARY'S THEOLOGY

This chapter, like the one on epistemology, will be short, and for the same reason: most of the points that could have been classified as belonging in this chapter have already been made in the previous one. The most important points of Mary's theology, of her philosophy ("love of wisdom", remember!) about God, have already been dealt with in chapter 3, where we unearthed some of the implied general principles of her metaphysics from her distinctively Jewish idea of God and her uniquely perfect response to Him.

But there are also a few other important points of philosophical theology to see implied in what we know about Mary: (1) God's existence, (2) how we can know it, (3) God's nature, (4) the problem of evil, (5) God's relationship to creation (6) and to us, (7) miracles, and (8) Divine Providence.

1. God's Existence

The first question rational theologians like Aquinas deal with is whether God exists or not. If the answer is "not", then theology itself becomes impossible, as physics becomes impossible for a philosopher who does not believe matter exists and as angelology becomes silly superstition for one who believes angels do not really exist.

Not only Mary, but most Jews, and in fact most human

beings until very recently, did not doubt that God existed. The only time the question of the existence of God is raised anywhere in the Bible is the dismissive line in the Psalms: "The fool says in his heart, 'There is no God'" (14:1a). From the Bible's point of view, atheism is an option only for fools, and fools are defined by their hearts, not just their minds; that is, by their sinful wills (14:1b). They have no light because they hate the light (Jn 3:19–21).

This strikes us as harsh, simplistic, and judgmental, but really, the only question is: Is it true?

Romans 1:18–32 identifies the psychological origin of atheism, not as a logical error, but as sinful behavior, especially sexual immorality. (That diagnosis is quite irrelevant to our culture, of course.) The whole point of the Bible is to tell us not what we already know by natural reason if we are not fools (that God is real), but what we do not know unless we believe what God tells us by supernatural revelation (that He loves us and saves us).

Of all the many great philosophical questions, this one— does God exist?—makes the most difference to everything else, to the whole meaning of life. Put the idea of God on one side of an idea-scale and every other idea that has ever entered the mind of man on the other side, and this one will outweigh all the others, as infinity outweighs everything finite. And yet, in a supreme irony, this question— is God real?—of all the great philosophical questions is the one Mary would simply laugh at. She would not search for proofs or worry about not finding one. She has no time for fools.

As I said above, this strikes us as harsh, simplistic, and judgmental. But is it *true*?

2. How We Can Know God

If an atheist were to ask Mary why she believes God exists and how the atheist could become convinced that he is wrong, it is possible to give a reasonable guess as to what her reply would be. Most likely, it would be a single world: "Pray." Or: "Love." Love your neighbor as if he were a beloved child of God. Then you will see that he is. This is how Dostoyevsky answered the question in *The Brothers Karamazov*, through his hero Father Zossima. Mary would answer the question by questioning the question. She would see the question as something like: "Why do you believe there is such a thing as the sun?" The answer is: "Look."

She would probably see the question as something as unnatural and strange as the question that many philosophers ask today: "Why do you believe there are not just knowable objects, material things like bodies and brains, but also knowing subjects, persons, selves, souls, or minds that think about matter and material things like bodies and brains? Why do you think that the thing that is thinking about its body right now is not just that body? Why do you think the word 'I' has any meaning at all?" The answer is as monosyllabic as Mary's "Pray." It is: "Think." Only when you stop thinking about the fact that you are thinking can you think that there is no thinking self. Only when you stop praying do you stop knowing God; only when you stop looking do you stop seeing sunlight.

3. The Nature of God and the Problem of Evil

Scripture does not waste time trying to prove God's existence, because that is not news to anyone but fools. What is news is the nature of God. God is love. God loves us. That is the surprising Good News.

It is far from obvious. The author of Ecclesiastes, who is neither a fool nor a wise man, but a philosopher, is the only writer in Scripture who uses only reason and sense observation and not faith; and he comes to the conclusion that human life is "vanity of vanities, all is vanity" (until the last few verses, where either he or a second author finally contradicts it) because although he admits that God exists, he does not see Him as knowable or trustable, and apparently not even good or just, since we find in His creation here both justice and injustice, both good and evil, in fact, two kinds of evil, both moral evil (sin) and physical evil (suffering and death). If the all-powerful God is good, why is there evil?

I have put these two questions, the nature of God and the problem of evil, together because it is only the belief that God's nature is neither "beyond good and evil" nor half good and half evil but totally good that seems contradicted by the existence of evil. The existence of evil is easily compatible with the existence of the pantheistic "Force" of *Star Wars* or an impersonal "cosmic consciousness" or with the equally impersonal and distant "snob God" of deism. It is the good, just, and loving God of the Bible that seems contradicted by the existence of evil.

Mary's answer to this problem of philosophical theology, "the problem of evil", is a "leap" of faith or free choice of the will rather than a logical argument. But it is evidence-based. It is based on the same empirical data on which the Jews have always based their faith: history, the past, God's great deeds of salvation as recounted in their tradition, written and oral. The prophets and the psalms love to repeat the story over and over. That is what their Scriptures are all about: the events, the data, the narrative, the story, the history: "His story". Thus Mary addresses God, in her Magnificat, as "my Savior", and recounts what He has done in the past to deserve that title. She sees His foot in the shape of His footprints in the sands of time. It is the most concrete possible answer to the problem of evil; God does not explain evil; He saves us from it, delivers us out of it.

The most important problem of evil is the practical one, not the theoretical one. The theoretical problem of evil is why it exists, how it could have arisen. It is about the past. The practical problem of evil is what to do about it. It is about the future and the present. Mary's scriptural data has just one chapter (Gen 3) about the first problem but thousands of chapters about the second. It includes both what God is doing about it and what we are supposed to be doing about it. What we are supposed to be doing about it is very clear: the two great Commandments summarize it. What God is doing about it is very mysterious.

The answer to the theoretical question is much more mysterious than the answer to the practical question. How was it possible for us (both in Adam and in ourselves) to be so stupid, in fact, so insane, as to prefer the foolishness of following our own imperfect will, with the misery that always eventually brings, to the wisdom of following God's perfect will, with the joy that always eventually brings? Mary's only answer to that theoretical question about wisdom and foolishness is a practical one: to practice the "love of wisdom" instead of the love of folly. She does not need to explain why the rest of us do not. To know sanity by practice is more important than to know insanity by theory.

Is that disappointing? If you could have only one of those two things, which one would you choose? The practical answer or the theoretical one? To whom would you rather listen, a perfect philosopher or a perfect saint? Whom would you rather be?

~

Mary's answer to the problem of evil is not rational theology but personal faith and trust. Yet this trust is utterly reasonable, for if God exists at all, and deserves the name, He must have at least three divine attributes: unlimited goodness, unlimited power, and unlimited wisdom. God cannot be wicked, weak, or stupid. Thus, He wills what is best for us, has the power to attain it, and knows the best way to do so. (And, of course, we do not know that, as He does, because we are not He [Quick! Call the reporters!], so His ways are bound to appear mysterious to us. That is the only "answer" to the problem of evil given in the Book of Job.)

This belief in a God who is all-good, all-powerful, and all-knowing, this refusal to call God one of the pagan gods, i.e., someone who is wicked, weak, and/or stupid, has a startling logical consequence. It is the most amazing verse in the Bible; it is the most unbelievable good news that we have ever heard: that God works all things together for good —all things, even evil things—for those who love Him and trust Him (Rom 8:28). That is Mary's wisdom about the problem of evil. Allowing evil is part of God's plan. Why does He do this? For some greater good. But we are not yet at the end of the play but in the middle, so we do not usually see that good, that end, that divine strategy. Of course not. We are not God. (Did those reporters get here yet?)

That is Mary's philosophical wisdom, Mary's answer to the hardest of all problems, the problem of evil.

Of course, Mary is an "amateur" rather than a "professional" philosopher. A professional lover of wisdom is a professional lover, and "a professional lover" is another word for "a prostitute", which is exactly the opposite of what she is.

Although her solution to this most basic of all human and all religious problems is practical rather than theoretical, we can summarize the more "theoretical" or systematic or properly theological answer to it very briefly if we keep her in mind. I shall do so now in less than one page.

There are two kinds of evil: the evil we do (moral evil) and the evil we suffer (physical evil and emotional evil). The problem of moral evil is easy to solve. Moral evil is not God's doing at all, but ours. Our power of free will, or free choice, is the only thing that could cause it. Why, then, does God not remove this dangerous power from us? Because free will is also the only thing that can cause love, and love is everything; love is the whole meaning of life; love is the very essential life of God.

The problem of the other kind of evil, suffering, however, is much more mysterious. Fortunately, it is also less important. Moral evil is more evil than physical or emotional evil. Sin is worse than suffering. Christ endured the lesser evil, on the Cross, to take away the greater evil. He endured temporal death in his body to save us from eternal death in our souls. For "what does it profit a man if he gain the whole world but lose his own soul?"

Let's think deeply and metaphysically about suffering. Suffering happens in time. Time permeates our whole life, spiritual as well as physical, our souls as well as our bodies. Time has three dimensions—past, present, and future—and therefore suffering, too, has those three dimensions. So the answer to the problem of suffering must have those three dimensions, too.

The three dimensions of our life in time may be symbolized by a room with two doors, an entrance and an exit. The entrance to our life in this world is birth, and its exit is death. Before we entered conscious time, we were in our mother's womb, which was like the Garden of Eden: we did not experience any suffering because we did not experience time, because time appears in our consciousness only when a gap appears between what we want and what we have, and that gap did not appear until birth and its trauma. So the first stage of our life, which is now past, had a different kind of time than what we experience now: Edenic time, time without suffering. The third stage, which is our future life after death, will also have a different kind of time because time as we experience it now is relative to the universe of space and matter and our material body, but after death we are no longer in this universe.

So Eden, History, and Heaven (or Hell) are our three stages.

Mary's answer to suffering and evil in the first stage is her Immaculate Conception in her mother's womb, which is of course a unique supernatural miracle and grace. It is not "Mary's answer", as if she invented it, but God's answer, which He invented in her. She is only His art, not the artist.

Mary's answer during her life is all concentrated in her *fiat*, as the whole universe was contained in the incredibly tiny thing that exploded in the Big Bang. Her "let it be" to the redemption echoes God's "let it be" to the creation.

And her answer after death is her Assumption into Heaven and her being crowned Queen of Heaven. And this too is not her answer but God's. She *is* His answer.

But *we* are not immaculately conceived, and we do not love God with all our heart, and we are not assumed into Heaven to be its queen. How does this apply to us?

We also acquire immaculate souls, by grace, through faith and Baptism. Mary is ahead of us on the road, but it is the same road.

We also can love God and neighbor in this life as what Karl Rahner has called our "fundamental option". That is why we will go to Heaven. But we do not do it with our whole heart, like Mary. That is why we will go through Purgatory first. Mary is ahead of us on this road, but it is the same road. She is "full" of the very same grace that will save us even though it is not yet in us as totally full.

We also hope to be taken to Heaven, though not as she was, immediately, in body and soul. She goes ahead of us on the road, but it is our road, too.

Now let us look at this life only, this life in time. Within this middle stage, i.e., within the time and history we now experience, there are also three sub-stages regarding any experience of suffering: the entrance door, the room (the experience of the suffering), and the exit door. Thus there are three questions about our present suffering:

(1) Why does God open the entrance door?
(2) What does He do to us when we are in the suffering room, on His operating table?
(3) What does He do to get us out of the exit door?

The first question amounts to why God does not let us live untroubled lives, why He does not prevent suffering, at least great suffering, from touching us, from opening the entrance door into our lives. He could do that without taking away our free will, it seems—although we would not be nearly *as* free or as strong or as fruitful or as loving or as holy, so that is a partial answer, and one that is well known by both tradition and experience.

But the ultimate reason God deliberately lets sufferings enter our lives is that we *need* to suffer, and we need to suffer because we are stupid, selfish sinners. We need rehab. God's reason for not removing all suffering is not merely that we *deserve* to suffer, in justice. That is quite true, but God could and does go beyond justice to mercy and forgiveness. Nor is His reason merely that suffering and death are the natural and necessary consequences of sin, though that is true, too. The body and the feelings necessarily suffer for the sins of the will because we are one thing, not two. But the main reason we need to suffer is God's mercy and love and compassion. If we sinned but never suffered the consequences, we would become totally spoiled brats in Hell forever. If we did not suffer, we would become insufferable. If you think that is unduly dark, hang around with Hollywood billionaires for a few years. Or take care of a two-year-old 24/7.

His subjective motive is love. His objective end is our perfection. The ultimate reason for suffering in stage two, the thing God uses it for, is to transform us into Christ, who is not only our Savior but also our model, our end, our goal, our perfection in humanity. He came among us, not just to take away our punishment, but to take away our sins, to make us saints. And He came, not to take away our sufferings, but to transform them into means of our sanctification. His death was our justification, but salvation is not just justification, freedom from punishment; it is also sanctification, freedom from sin. The angel said He would be called "Jesus", i.e., "Savior", not because He would save us from the punishment for our sins, but because "He will save us from our *sins*."

And the third part of the answer is repeated literally thousands of times in Scripture: in words of petition for deliverances future that are based on praise for deliverances past, especially in the Psalms; and in words of promise of that future deliverance in the Epistles. Our hope is based on God's data, on God's deeds, not just on His words. The Exodus is archetypal here. Although God leads us into Egypt and into slavery and into oppression and into suffering and into the sea and even into "the valley of the shadow of death" (the sea is a natural image of death), yet He also leads us out. He is the Master of both doors.

Although we suffer, if we suffer in faith, in trust, in love, in Him, as part of His Body, our suffering will produce far greater joy in the end. We can say by faith now what we will say by understanding in the end: "Thanks, I needed that." We do not see this end yet, but we certainly can believe it, because God Himself tells this to us again and again in Scripture and in the teachings and lives of the saints.

And we all are given little hints and glimpses of it even now. That awful physical or emotional pain that threw us for a loop in the past—it made us stronger and wiser and humbler, didn't it? We do not see that for all sufferings, or even for most, but we see it for some, so it is possible that God is at work doing it for all of our sufferings. It is not provable, but it is believable. It is a Pascal's "wager". One we cannot lose but only win.

To change the image from the gambling table to the battlefield, we are at war. Although we struggle against and often succumb to our enemies (which are evil spirits and their spies and colonies in our hearts, the sins to which they tempt us), we are always also saved from them. There is an exit door as well as an entrance door. We lose many battles, but we will win the war, if only we trust and obey our Commanding Officer.

So God (1) does not prevent suffering by locking the entrance door.

But He (2) transforms its meaning into an ontologically real participation in (and not just a psychological imitation of) Christ and His sufferings (see Col 1:24), which makes us gradually into little Christs. It is an operation. "The wounded surgeon plies the steel" (T. S. Eliot).

And (3) as He delivered Christ by resurrection and ascension, He does the same to us.

The very best and most incredible piece of Good News —that we are "very members incorporate in the Mystical Body of [His] Son" (to quote the *Book of Common Prayer*) is also the reason for our sufferings. They are His work, His mission, and therefore ours. That "therefore" justifies anything. It is far better to be with Christ on His Cross than to be without Him anywhere else. It is better to be in love in the South Bronx than to be divorced in Hawaii.

Where does Mary come in here? To answer that question, take a good, long look at the *Pietà*, with both your mind and your eyes. (The eyes of the mind and the eyes of the body are like the two blades of a pair of scissors. They cut much deeper and better together than apart.) Mary's sufferings were far greater than ours. And her free unlocking and unqualified *fiat* to His will was also far greater than ours. But she is ahead of us on the very same road. We are to grow increasingly like her: we are to be active operators, or rather cooperators, in the work of our own redemption. And others' too, in "the Communion of Saints", for every good work we do aids all the members in the Body of Christ, while every sin we commit harms all the other members, too.

That cooperation is the point of her title "Co-Redemptrix". It is ours, too. She is our mother and our model to imitate, not a goddess on a pedestal to stare at. God gave her to us, not to swoon in her shadow, but to climb in her light. (The arresting image is from Teilhard de Chardin's *The Divine Milieu*.) What God accomplished through her, through her free *fiat*, through her enabling and cooperating with Christ's sufferings, is a far greater feat than what He ever accomplished through any other merely human being. In fact, it is even greater than the work of creating the universe, for the universe put up no obstacles to His work, as we do. Mary did not.

Chapter VI

MARY'S COSMOLOGY

Cosmology means, of course, a *logos* (rational account) of the "cosmos" (order of the world or the universe). Many of the questions premodern philosophers debated in cosmology have since been answered by modern science, but not by any means all of them, especially the questions about the cosmos that are about its relation to God and His activity in it.

God's Relationship to Creation

The most important question in cosmology is the relation between the cosmos and God.

That is true, but that very way of putting the problem is pagan rather than Jewish: putting the cosmos first and looking at God from its standpoint implicitly looks at the cosmos as the standard and looks at God as relative to it rather than vice versa. The question for Judaism is, first of all, about God and His relation to the creation, not about the creation and its relation to God. The very word for it changes, from "the cosmos" to "the creation", reversing the mental relationship between these two concepts and putting everything in its place, relativizing the relative and absolutizing the absolute.

But the other question, from the pagan point of view, the question about the cosmos rather than about God, is important, too, for it distinguishes supernaturalism ("There is More") from naturalism ("This is all there is"). In Mary's biblical imagination, the whole cosmos is a Jacob's ladder, with God or His angels ascending and descending on it like trucks on a highway. For this biblical cosmology, the world and life are a ladder connecting us to God and God to us. And the identity of this ladder is finally revealed in the New Testament to mean—nothing less than Mary's Son, who uses the exact words of the Genesis story of Jacob's ladder (Gen 28:12) to refer to Himself (Jn 1:51).

This view of the *cosmos* as a ladder entails a view of *life* as one. Mary saw everything that existed in God's creation and everything that His will brought into her life as relative to the two persons they connected, herself and God. The only two persons you can never, for a second, either in time or eternity, escape are God and yourself. You are made in His image; that is why you call yourself by the same absolutely unique pronoun, "I". Everything in the cosmos He designed exists for that relationship. The cosmos is the setting for the play, and the plot is your relationship, first, with God and, then, with His other images. The whole cosmos is like a tube. The tube is infinitely large at God's end and very, very tiny at yours. God comes into the tube at His end and out of it at yours. That is Mary's cosmology.

It is unique to Mary in one way: in that the Creator came not only into her life and her will but also into her body. But since the body is an image of the soul, and since God wants to come into your soul as He came into Mary's, she is our model here, too. The angel's message to her is also to us, though in a different way: "The Holy Spirit will come upon you, and the power of the Most High will overshadow you; therefore that child to be born will be called holy, the Son of God." The same One Who entered Mary's body must enter our soul if we are to be saved. Our *fiat* must echo hers. Life is antiphony, and Mary sings the first part.

~

To appreciate the distinctiveness of Mary's cosmology, we need to contrast her Jewish tradition with the pagan Greek (and then Roman) tradition.

The Greeks were cosmocentric; the Jews were theocentric. The Greeks saw their gods as relative to the cosmos, i.e., the ordered whole that we call the "universe". They were on top, man was in the middle (in "middle-earth"), and everything else was at the bottom (also in a hierarchy, from unordered matter through ordered matter, to plants, lower animals, and higher animals).

If "gods" are replaced by "angels", this picture is quite right. But the *frame* is wrong. The Jews reversed the relationship between God and the cosmos. God defined the cosmos, not vice versa. In paganism, the gods were defined by their place in the cosmic whole. They were not totally transcendent, for the so-called "creation myths" ("sacred stories") were really only formation myths. The concept of creation proper, i.e., creation by a single, eternal, omnipotent God, out of no preexisting material, out of nothing, is distinctively Jewish. Thus, the "cosmos" is now relative to the Creator in its very being. He gave it not only order but existence.

This new theology results in a new cosmology. The world is neither secular nor sacred. It is not a purely accidental and random batch of colliding atoms, and neither is it the holy house or bodily dwelling of the gods, who in paganism live, not outside the universe, but in it, in sacred clouds, trees, mountains, storms, rocks, and so forth, and above all in wooden or stone idols.

Mary's cosmology is as distinctively Jewish as her theology. For its God is both more transcendent *and* more immanently and actively present to the cosmos than in paganism.

One of the great questions in theology is God's relationship to His creation. The two obvious options are immanence or transcendence, pantheism or deism, here or there, inside or outside the box. This makes the box, i.e., the cosmos, the standard and asks where God is relative to the box: inside or outside. Pantheists, both monotheists and polytheists, say "inside", and deists say "outside". Religious Jews, like Mary, opt for a third option, which repudiates both deism and pantheism. For the god of deism is too far away to be our Savior, and the god of pantheism is too involved in evil to be our Savior from it, for he is indifferent to good or evil, like an all-encompassing, shapeless blob. Deism's god is a snob, and pantheism's god is a blob.

Mary's God is both immanent (present to His creation, though not confined to it) and transcendent (more than the whole of creation, though not distant and absent from it). That is a paradox. But here are three analogies to it:

(1) Light, which transcends all colors and shapes, can be totally present to and illumine all colors and shapes, as no color or shape can do without obliterating all other colors or shapes.

(2) The mind, which is not any material object, can know all material objects, making any and all of them present in itself like a mirror.

(3) There is also an analogy in metaphysics: existence, which transcends all finite and definable essences, actualizes every essence that is made actual rather than only potential. Existence makes actual all essences from within, so to speak.

Peel off the accidental, external layers of any being one by one, and you come to its existence at its very center, which actualizes its essence, its essential properties, its natural but changeable properties, its accidental properties, its activities, and its relationships to other things. Existence actualizes every one of these layers, not from without, as the supreme accident, but from within. (Of course "within" is only a metaphor; existence is not confined to space.) Existence is the supreme actuality; mere essences are only potential to existence. Saint Thomas gives us what Gilson called "the great syllogism" to summarize this:

> MAJOR PREMISE: Being (existence) is that which is most intimately present and central to everything. (It is the supreme actuality, that which makes anything that is real to be real.)
>
> MINOR PREMISE: God is infinite existence itself, unlimited by and transcendent to every finite essence.
>
> CONCLUSION: God is most intimate, present, and central to all things. He is most imminent precisely because He is most transcendent (like light to color or mind to things).

Mary did not think in such abstract terms as essence and existence or in such logical forms as syllogisms, but she did know God as the Creator, the giver of existence itself, and that is why she saw God in all things. This was the theology and, therefore, the cosmology that Christians inherited from the Jews, our fathers in the faith. As the old hymn says:

> Thy bountiful care what tongue can recite?
> It breathes in the air, it shines in the light;
> It streams from the hills, it descends to the plain,
> And sweetly distills in the dew and the rain.

Of the many gods or versions of God in the history of human thought, only one is both fully transcendent and fully immanent. For human reason, left to itself and its dependence on the imagination, is impaled on the dilemma of Here or There, Home or Away, Inside or Outside, Pantheism or Deism, Whole or Part. It is natural and easy to affirm either one of these two opposite ideas, and almost impossible to affirm both of them at once—and, even more paradoxically, for the very same reason: to see that it is God's most extreme possible transcendence that allows for His most extreme possible immanence, as in the three analogies above.

This cosmology of seeing God's presence in all things does not rival or crush or erase nature's reality or value or specific details, as one might expect. Just the opposite: as light makes colors brighter, not dimmer, the Creator makes the creation brighter, not dimmer. For the Author does not rival either the characters or the setting of His epic drama that is the history of the universe and of human life. It is no accident that a ridiculously large proportion of the world's great scientists, doctors, and artists are Jews.

~

The paradox of immanence and transcendence has obvious religious as well as cosmological consequences. Mary addresses God as "my Savior". Only the God of the Bible can deserve that title. The god of deism is not present—his arm does not reach to earth—and the god of pantheism is not transcendent—his arm cannot deliver from evil because it is equally present in evil as well as good. God cannot save you from part of Himself.

The consequences of this cosmology are, as usual, intensely practical. Since God is present, not absent, a religion, i.e., a lived relationship with God, consists first of all of practicing that presence, as Brother Lawrence puts it with wonderful simplicity in his little classic *The Practice of the Presence of God*. This is very similar to what is often identified as the heart of Jesuit spirituality, finding God in all things.

The cosmological point is not just philosophical, it is also religious. Air, space, and time are all present to us also, but they cannot save us or know us or love us. God is more than just *present*, He is *personally* present, present as a Person, a Knower and Lover. This is religion rather than theology, but it is based on the theology of the rejection of both pantheism and deism, neither of which allows the transcendent personal Creator to be present, especially present as Person to persons, what Buber calls the "I-Thou" relationship. Thus this religious relationship assumes the theology that sees personhood ("I AM") as God's supreme perfection. (See the previous section on "The Metaphysics of I AM" pp. 131–34.) What is present is a Person, not a Force; a "He", not an "It".

This is not unique to Mary, but it is unique to Judaism and Christianity; and at the Annunciation, Mary is the fulfillment of all of Judaism. She is all of Judaism at its point, like an arrow's point entering its predestined target. She is the representative of the whole cosmos; she is the summit of the cosmic mountain God created.

2. Miracles

One of the classic questions in cosmology is whether nature is open or closed to supernatural miracles. If there is a God who is both transcendently omnipotent and immanently present and active in the world, miracles can happen.

Mary implicitly asked for a miracle at Cana and trusted her divine Son to perform one, and she got it. Implied in this event are a number of other theological assumptions that are relevant to miracles: (a) the power of intercession, (b) God's use of His faithful creatures as instruments, and (c) God's compassionate care about the daily problems of His children. All three are examples of the previous point. Neither the God of deism nor the God of pantheism performs miracles.

Implied is also the principle that theologians formulate in such words as these: divine grace does not neglect, ignore, demean, rival, or bypass created nature but uses it and perfects it and glorifies it. God is not a micro-manager but exalts His subordinates.

Mary saw at least five great miracles, and probably more. They were (1) the Virgin Birth, (2) Elizabeth's postmenopausal pregnancy, (3) Christ's first public miracle of changing water to wine at the wedding feast at Cana, (4) the Resurrection, and (5) Pentecost. She probably saw many more, for if she had not seen Jesus perform miracles before, she would probably not have expected one at Cana.

Mary saw nature as open to supernature, as the moon is open to meteorites from above making craters on its surface. Her history was pockmarked with "miracle craters". At the very center of her whole religion was sacred history. Her Scriptures were divided into three parts: the historical books, the wisdom books, and the prophetic books, and the historical ones came first in the Bible because they came first in importance. The same is true of the New Testament. And at the heart of both histories there are miracles, because history is His story.

To believe in God but not miracles is to reduce God to

either the "snob God" of deism, the absentee landlord or deadbeat dad who brings no surprises to his kids, or the "blob God" of pantheism, which is simply "All There Is" and therefore not "more". A hurricane is like a miracle to the land because the land cannot produce waves of water from within itself; thus pantheism excludes miracles. If pantheism is true and God is Everything and Everything is God, then by the very definition of a miracle, there can be no miracles. Nothing comes from outside because there is no "outside" to Everything.

3. Divine Providence

Mary's total trust, expressed in her *fiat* to God's angel, is based on her faith in Divine Providence. And this faith, in turn, is based on the theology at the heart of Judaism, namely, the self-revealed divine name of JHWH, "I AM WHO I AM." To see the connection, remember that this can equally be translated as "I WILL BE WHAT I WILL BE." There is no distinction between the present tense and the future tense in the Hebrew word. Thus "I will be what I will be" implies "Trust Me. Your life is designed by My perfect will for you and your future."

This implies a number of theological assumptions, especially

(a) God's eternity and, thus, His omniscience: He knows as present what to us is future;

(b) God's goodwill to provide what is best for us;

(c) God's power and control over all of His creation; and

(d) the need for faith, because to us God is surprising and unpredictable since we are not omniscient but He is. Two things are certain: that we do not always understand what He is doing, since we are not God, and that He certainly does, since He is!

(e) It also implies the need for the virtue of hope, for this faith of ours, though not provable now, will be proved by facts, by the future, by God's *emeth*, His faithfulness in keeping His promises. That Hebrew word (*emeth*) is also translated as "truth". Truth "happens".

No more spectacular example of all these principles exists in history than Mary's relationships to God as His faithful daughter, as the faithful mother of His incarnate Son, and as the faithful spouse of His Spirit. All three relationships are relationships of faith in and faithfulness to God's perfect Providence.

4. *Angels*

Angels are not part of the material universe, but they are part of the cosmos, or the created order, so they are part of cosmology. "Angelology", the philosophical and theological science of angels, is not a common word. You have probably never heard it before. But it is a perfectly right division of philosophy, a subdivision of cosmology. And it is necessary because (1) angels really exist and (2) are neither divine nor human nor subhuman.

They are excluded by current secular assumptions and ideologies. But they are not excluded by science. Science can say nothing about them, any more than fish, if they were scientists, could say anything about airplanes. They are not excluded by philosophy, for there are no good rational arguments against them and one at least very probable rational argument for them, namely, the empirical observation of the plethora of creatures below us on the great chain of being, the divine creativity they manifest, and the metaphysical possibility of their inhabiting the place between us and God, Who is infinite spirit. They are finite spirits without bodies. We are finite spirits ensouled in bodies. Animals are bodies with feeling souls but not rational souls (spirits). Plants are bodies with growing souls but not feeling souls or rational souls. Everything else that we know of in the universe is bodies without souls or spirits, from atoms to galaxies.

Angels, like prophets and like miracles, fit into God's non-deistic policy of active involvement in the cosmos. God uses angels as instruments, messengers, and mediators of His mind and will and power to mankind. Angels are semi-transcendent: they are superhuman but subdivine. God used one (Gabriel) for His most important encounter with mankind: the one with Mary, the one on which everyone's salvation depended. If angels have spiritual emotions like awe and wonder and fear, try to imagine Gabriel's awe at Mary, his wonder at God, and his fear that her free will might not say "Yes" to God's free offer to redeem mankind from eternal death. Angels do not infallibly know the future. Has any artist ever captured that awe, wonder, and fear on Gabriel's face at the Annunciation?

Angelology is as legitimate and independent a division of human thinking as zoology or botany or physics; but since it is "under" (as part of) theology on the great chain of being, it is usually classified "under" theology in arranging the sciences. Angels are not gods or God, of course, but they are pure spirits, like God. There are no bodies above us humans and no spirits below us on the chain. We are the only beings in all reality that are both physical and spiritual. We are the cosmological amphibians.

If you clipped out of the Bible all mention of angels and all events in which angels are active, you would have something that looked more like the contents of a wastebasket than a book.

Mary did not doubt or question Gabriel or the truth and trustability of his message to her. How many theologians would do the same if addressed by an angel with such startling words?

When the angel came to Mary, this did not at all upset her world view, her cosmology. Angels had flown into and out of her Scriptures, her tradition, and her history like thunderstorms, and Mary accepted both as equally real parts of God's cosmos and actions. The only surprise, because of her humility, was that the angel should pick her out. She is also troubled because she knows that angels, like miracles, appear only at moments of crisis.

It is also significant that the angel has to say "fear not." Real angels do that; fake angels do not. No Hallmark greeting-card angel ever says "fear not."

What the Annunciation tells us about Mary's cosmology is that her world, unlike our modern one, was not a locked iron vault but a semipermeable membrane through which angels leaked, in a spiritual osmosis. (I always liked the name "Angelique": it sounds like "angel leak".) Mary's world was not a flat, one-story ranch house but a skyscraper, a Jacob's ladder.

I wonder: How often have we (have I?) forgotten, ignored, denied, distrusted, or dismissed angels who visited us invisibly with inspirations? For every visible appearance of an angel, there are probably millions of invisible visits. Anonymity is their preferred *modus operandi*. They are humble.

~

Mary's wisdom, always practical, tells us a number of distinctive, practical things about angels, all of them in her brief encounter with Gabriel in the Annunciation (Lk 1:26–38):

(1) Acknowledge their reality. Do not think you are hallucinating. Do not protest, in the face of an angel, that he can be explained psychologically. Fit your world into his; do not try to fit his into yours. Yours is a lot narrower than his.

(2) Be reverent. Have holy fear. For you are to him as a tiny, fragile animal is to you.

(3) Pay close attention to his message. He is a messenger. That is the meaning of the word "angel" and his job description. If it is perilous to ignore a message from the IRS, it is even more perilous to ignore a message from an angel or to "reinterpret" or "nuance" its message if it surprises, puzzles, or upsets you.

(4) But it is perfectly proper to ask the angel questions, in the spirit of a slow and stupid student questioning his wise and patient professor.

(5) Ask questions especially if the angel's words seem to put into question a solemn vow you made to God.

(6) Question in faith, not in doubt. Believe the angel. Angels never lie. That is what demons do. God does not like it if you confuse His angel with a demon. Zechariah, the priest and the husband of Mary's cousin Elizabeth, was rendered deaf and dumb for nine months for doubting an angel (Lk 1:5–25, 57–66). Mary never doubted, she only wondered and pondered.

(7) "Trust *and obey*, for there is no other way."

(8) Begin your obedience in your will's free choice (Mary's *fiat*), which angels, like God, always respect. They are gentlemen, not bullies.

(9) Speak your obedience. Words have power.

(10) Where angels gather, devils will come. Life is spiritual warfare. Herod's massacre of the babies and the Holy Family's flight into Egypt and exile is an example of this. (See Revelation 12.)

5. The Face of the Cosmos

There is one more point about Mary's cosmology, and it is both the most surprising and the most important. Behind everything in the cosmos, Mary saw a Face.

The cosmos is like a puzzle, like one of those old-fashioned puzzles for kids in Sunday newspapers: "Find the face in the picture." Another version was "connect the dots." Mary connected the dots and saw the face of God hiding behind everything. That is the ultimate meaning of the cosmos: it is God's mask.

It is the mask of the Father, the invisible One Who created the visible world through His *Logos*, His Word. The eyes of the body do not see Him, but the eyes of the soul, which are the eyes of faith and hope and love, do.

This Word also hid in Mary's womb, behind a real human nature, both soul and body. This meant that the secret of Mary's philosophical anthropology (our next topic), Mary's answer to our great question "Know thyself", or "What is Man, that Thou art mindful of him?" was not a "show and tell" but just a "show". It was not an abstract idea or definition but a concrete Person, Jesus. Her answer to that great question ("What is Man?") is also her answer to our prayer to her that she loves the most: "Show unto us the blessed fruit of thy womb." There is nothing she loves to do more than that.

The answer to the question "What is man?" is the same as the answer to the question "What is God?" It is Christ. He reveals us to ourselves, as well as revealing God to us. He is the nature of man, the meaning of man, the identity God designed for all of us. He is Perfect Man as well as Perfect God, and Mary can show Him to us best because she is perfect woman.

He was hiding His divinity there, as He still does in the Eucharist, where He also hides His humanity. The word for "hiding" (*latens, latitat*) is used twice in the first verse of Saint Thomas' great Eucharistic hymn. He is not just *there*; He is active, acting, doing something: He is hiding, as He did in her womb.

And the Holy Spirit Whom He sent, Whom Mary received at Pentecost, *His* Spirit, is also hiding in the Church. He is the soul of the Church. He is to the Church what our souls are to our bodies.

Symbolically, Mary is the Church. Saint John Paul II said that "the Marian dimension of the Church is prior to the Petrine." He is even harder to see there, because this divine organism looks very much like a merely human organization. It looks like "organized religion", or, often more like disorganized religion. It is manned by jackasses, but it still carries Christ, as one once did into Jerusalem. Its bishops include Judas Iscariot and his spiritual descendants. Its faithful (us) are shallow, selfish, stupid, sinful schmucks much of the time. It is about these schmucks, and not just about its super saints and holy heroes, that our Lord said:

"What you do to the least of these, My brethren, you do to Me."

Mary's cosmology is an anthropology because she saw the face in the picture.

Chapter VII

MARY'S ANTHROPOLOGY

1. The Question

"Know thyself", said Socrates, echoing the Delphic oracle, the greatest religious authority in his culture. He did not mean "Know your unique personality and personal desires", but "Know what and why you are", "Know the meaning of life", "Know what is the essence and end (Aristotle called it the formal cause and the final cause) of human existence."

As usual, contemporary philosophers tend to ignore this large and human question and try to imitate the sciences in narrowing their focus to questions like brain vs. mind, whether consciousness is epiphenomenal or substantial, or questions of racial, economic, and gender "identity". There is at least one question to which they give a very clear answer: why philosophy in particular and the humanities in general are in such radical decline today.

Like Socrates, Pascal did not ignore the big question. Unlike Socrates, Pascal found the complete answer and found it outside himself. I think if he were allowed to pick any one of his 1000 famous "Pensées" to inscribe on the minds of everyone on earth, it would be this one, because it gives the total, final, and definitive answer to the four greatest questions in the world:

"Without Jesus Christ, we do not know who we are or who God is. We do not know the meaning of our life or of our death. He who knows Him knows the reason for everything."

Mary knows the reason for everything. The reason for everything lived in her womb for nine months, in her life for thirty-three years, and in her heart forever.

2. *The Fundamental Answer*

The world finds that answer insufferably narrow and dogmatic. Yet it is the essential claim of Christianity. If it is not true, Christianity is a lie.

The favorite quotation, outside the Bible, of the greatest man of the worst century in history, Saint John Paul II, was Vatican II's maxim that "Christ reveals man to himself." He is the final and definitive answer to the two great questions of who God is and who man is. He is the totality and perfection of God and the totality and perfection of man. He is the totality of God because "in him all the fulness of God was pleased to dwell" (Col 1:19), so that He can truly say: "He who has seen me has seen the Father" (Jn 14:9). He is also the totality and perfection of man, so that in one stroke, He shows us the fullness of the only two persons we cannot avoid or escape for one instant in time or in eternity, God and ourselves.

Mary's whole ministry is to answer the prayer "Show us the blessed fruit of thy womb, Jesus", to bring Him into the world, first physically, in the Annunciation and the Nativity, then spiritually, in her continuing heavenly ministry and mission throughout our history.

This mission of hers is for us, not for her. This implies that the answer to the philosophical question of anthropology, "know thyself", or "what is man?" or "what is the human self?" is that it is essentially *relational*, like the Trinity. We are created in God's image, not our own; and we are destined for union with God, not with ourselves; and at every present moment, our whole definition and our whole destiny is in that relationship with Him and, in Him, with each other. It is not an addition; it is our essence. Without that twofold relationship, we are not something else; we are literally nothing at all. The title of Cardinal Sarah's first great book applies to us: *God or Nothing.*

In fact, not only are we wise and good and happy only in relation to God, but we are only *real* to the extent that we are rightly related to Him Who is the standard of reality as well as of truth and goodness and beauty, of wisdom and love and joy. The Supreme Being is the standard and touchstone of all being. Our deepest need and our deepest subconscious thirst are ontological. Our deep demand for more being is at the hidden heart of our demand for more truth and goodness and beauty and joy.

What were our remote ancestors seeking in all their myths and rituals? Why did they worship gods and heroes and fabled ancestors? Why did Plato divinize his "Ideas"? It was the thirst for being. Saints and sages and heroes and archetypes seemed more real than we are, and we seemed more real when we were in some kind of contact with them. There are degrees of reality. A saint is more real than a sinner, as a man is more real than a ghost.

Hindu psychology (which is far more profound than Hindu theology), based on thousands of years of inner searching, summarizes the innate and universal wants of the heart of man in four layers. Most obvious but also most ephemeral and external is the desire for pleasure, then power, then moral duty and service and virtue. But deepest of all is the desire for *sat, chit,* and *ananda,* which mean infinite being or life, infinite knowing or understanding, and infinite joy, which comes from love. Infinite joy (*ananda*) fulfills the heart, and infinite understanding (*chit*) fulfills the mind, but the first and deepest demand of all is infinite life, infinite being (*sat*). Our being is thin; we want it to be thicker. It is light, like a feather; we need it to be heavier, like a mountain. It is tiny, like a grain of sand; we want it to be great, like a galaxy. It is ephemeral, like grass; we want it to be eternal, like God.

Saint John the Evangelist uses essentially the same three concepts in his First Epistle (and in his Gospel, too) as *sat*, *chit*, and *ananda* in Hinduism: they are "life", "light", and "love". The "light" is more than photons; it is truth, of which sensible light is only a symbol. The "love" is *agape*, of which all other loves are only shadows. And the "life" is God's own life, *zoe*, not *bios*, supernatural and eternal life, not just natural and temporal life. *Bios* is not enough life even if that life is filled with a lot of truth and goodness.

Jesus speaks about this to Nicodemus: that we need to be "born again", to get a new being, a new life (not just a new life-style), which is *zoe*. We need, and deep down we want, even if we do not know that we want, nothing less than to share in the very life of God. We need "divinization", *theosis*, as the Eastern Orthodox put it. We need (and if we dare to be honest and wise, we want) a share in the very life of God.

That is not Oriental mysticism; that is biblical Christianity. Read 2 Peter 1:4.

We need a new identity. The very same point can be put in the apparently opposite way: we need to regain our true identity that we have lost, which is God's eternal design for us. I, this concrete individual in time, need to become one with God's eternal idea for me. In other words, we need to become what Mary is.

Our identity is our relation to God. Mary knew this. Her simple and direct answer to God's angel at the Annunciation proves that she knew it. Her answer is the answer to the central question of anthropology, "know thyself." She invites us to "behold" this answer: "Behold, I am the handmaid of the Lord" (Lk 1:38).

That is not just her *task*; it is her whole *identity*. There is no Mary outside that. She is essentially relational and, thereby, teaches us that we are, too. To be God's servant is to be truly free, free to be our true selves. We idolaters (our most popular idols are ourselves) often identify our very selves with our job, our gender, our ideology, our feelings, our sexual desires, or even our smartphones. We disappear into them. But Christ does not let us disappear when we come to Him. Light lets everything appear as it is, and He is the light of the world that alone lets us appear truly, as we really are, as God designed us to be. And He will not rest until He has made us to be *that*. That is why there is not only great suffering but also great joy in Purgatory: we are there becoming fully ourselves, like snakes shedding their dirty old skin.

There are only a few possible anthropologies. If our identity is not in our relation to God, it must find itself in its relation to something else. And there are only three or four alternatives there. Some see themselves in relation to no one but themselves. That is pretty much the definition of Hell. Some see themselves in relation to nature, as parts of nature, as randomly evolved star stuff. Nature is their only God. And some, perhaps most, see themselves in relation to other human beings. Their fundamental identity is in their family and friends or their identity group, their race, class, gender, or ideology; or their career or even their political party. Perhaps a few find their identity in something abstract. Even religion can degenerate into an abstraction, an idea.

So what are our choices?

First, there is no choice not to choose. For that is itself a choice, a self-refuting one.

Second, we cannot choose relativism instead of absolutism because that is to choose relativism as our absolute. We cannot avoid some absolute, some worship object.

And that can only be either God or some idol.

And the idols are also limited to three or four possibilities: self, nature, other people, or perhaps something abstract. We are in a drama, and we must take our bearings from the Author, ourselves, the other characters, the setting, or the theme.

Mary speaks for all religious people, at least all Christians, Jews, and Muslims, in her choice: "Behold, I am the handmaid of the Lord."

∼

What led Mary to say "Behold me"? Surely it was not her personal pride. There was 0 percent of that in her. It was its polar opposite, her humble, self-forgetful trust in her Heavenly Father's perfect love and wisdom and power, that is, it was what De Caussade calls her "abandonment to Divine Providence". There was 100 percent of that in her. She simply had no idea how famous she would become. She was so in love with God that she forgot herself completely and, therefore, pointed with joy to herself in exactly the same spirit as she would point to another recipient of God's grace: in the spirit that sees all persons, oneself and others, equally, as mirrors that reflect the same light or as transparent windows to look through, not as opaque objects to look at. That does not mean that she ignored the windows, i.e., the human beings in her life that reflected that light like stained glass, in differently beautiful ways. She saw the light *in* them as well as *through* them.

When she said, "Behold me", she was saying "Behold Him." She disappears like a perfectly clear window, and God appears in it. If you want to see the meaning of man, look at Mary. She is God's mirror. Even when she is saying "behold me", she is saying "Behold God." She is saying: "Look *along* me, not *at* me. Look at my looking. Follow my arrow to the target. I am only a finger, an arrow. The target is not the arrow. My whole being is to be a pointing finger. Don't sniff my finger like a dumb dog who cannot understand the meaning of signs. Look along my looking: look at Him. That is the way to 'know thyself.' You cannot know yourself unless you forget yourself."

The same principle applies to love of neighbor as applies to love of God. Once you love your neighbors as you love yourself, you can love yourself with the same self-forgetful love with which you love your neighbors. You can be your own neighbor. Saint Bernard of Clairvaux says there are four steps in loving God: you begin by loving yourself for your own sake; then you love God, but for your own sake, for what He can do for you; then you love God for His own sake; and then, finally, you can love even yourself for God's sake rather than for your own sake. Once you overcome selfishness, you can love even yourself unselfishly. Mary exemplifies this perfectly.

This is a consequence of man being made in God's image. The relation between God and man is like the relation between a person and his image in a mirror. In this life, God cannot be seen directly. He "dwells in inaccessible light".

He says "Man cannot see me and live" (Ex 33:20). But we can see what God is like, or rather what is like God, when we see saints, for they are the clearest mirrors, and they reflect His image best. Of course, we are all muddy mirrors, cracked and foggy, fallen and foolish. The only clear and immaculate mirror is the one God chose to be His mother.

3. Freedom and Destiny

One of the most obvious and popular philosophical puzzles is what William James called "the dilemma of determinism". It is a dilemma because nearly everyone instinctively senses both that there is freedom of will, especially in choosing between good and evil (if not, we are not responsible and it is meaningless to praise or blame anyone for anything), and also that life is meaningful, teleological, designed toward an end, a destiny. If not, then randomness rather than order reigns in reality, and all stories, which are mankind's oldest, most universal, and fundamental art form, systematically deceive.

But freedom and determinism contradict each other. That is the dilemma.

How does Mary solve it?

How did Julius Caesar solve it when he faced the apparent either/or dilemma of whether to cross the Rubicon River and march on Rome to transform the republic into an empire? The Senate, the supreme authority under the republic, had forbidden him to do it. His choice to obey or to disobey was totally up to him, totally free. Yet his explanation and justification for it was that it was his "destiny", his fate. It was his supreme necessity, and yet it was also supremely free. Did he solve the dilemma of determinism vs. free will, or did he dissolve it?

How did Martin Luther solve it when, at the Diet of Worms, accused of heresy (accurately!) and commanded to repent and abjure his heresy and submit to the pope, he freely chose to follow his conscience, instead, knowing that it would probably lead to his death. The choice was unpredictable and free; yet it was "fateful"—in fact, his famous words justifying it were strikingly similar to Caesar's: "Here I stand. I can do no other. God help me." Did he solve the dilemma of determinism, or did he dissolve it?

A third example of the same psychology of the unification of freedom and destiny (or, if you like, predestination) is C. S. Lewis, in his spiritual autobiography *Surprised by Joy*. Here is what he says about the moment of his choice to believe:

> I became aware that I was holding something at bay, or shutting something out. Or, if you like, that I was wearing some stiff clothing, like corsets, or even a suit of armor, as if I were a lobster. I felt myself being, there and then, given a free choice. I could open the door or keep it shut; I could unbuckle the armor or keep it on. . . . The choice appeared to be momentous but it was also strangely unemotional. I was moved by no desires or fears. In a sense I was not moved by anything. I chose to open, to unbuckle, to loosen the rein. I say, "I chose," yet it did not really seem possible to do the opposite. On the other hand, I was aware of no motives. You could argue that I was not a free agent, but I am more inclined to think that this came nearer to being a perfectly free act than most that I have ever done. Necessity may not be the opposite of freedom, and perhaps a man is most free when, instead of producing motives, he could only say, "I am what I do.". . . Freedom, or necessity? Or do they differ at their maximum? At that maximum a man is what he does; there is nothing of him left over or outside the act. As for what we commonly call Will, and what we commonly call Emotion, I

fancy these usually talk too loud, protest too much, to be quite believed.

The point is not that the justification for the choice was objectively true and correct in the case of either Caesar or Luther, as it was in the case of Lewis. In fact, believers in democracy say Caesar did the wrong thing in turning a republic into an empire, and Catholics say Luther chose the wrong theology instead of the right one. But both followed what they believed was their fate, their rightful destiny. Whatever the arguments, if any, that they used to justify their choice rationally or morally, the psychology was the same as that of C. S. Lewis' choice to become a Christian.

A fourth example of the same principle of free will and fate or necessity or destiny becoming identical can be seen in Frodo's heroic choice to save Middle-Earth by accepting the Quest to destroy the Ring of Power. At the Council of Elrond, he utters the quintessentially Marian words: "I will take the Ring, although I do not know the way."

And this was surely the same psychology we find in Mary's *fiat*, which was her infinitely fateful *and* free choice to accept her divinely predestined fate, the free choice on which hung all the world's hope of Heaven.

For the God who invented free will in His creatures, the God who, as Chesterton paradoxically put it, in doing so, "broke His own law and made a graven image of Himself", refused to save the world without our free cooperation. He gave Eve and Mary the same freedom and the same choice, with opposite results. He gave Christ the same choice; His human will was free, and, therefore, His temptations were real, not a fake, not a pretense like a play on stage, and not a mere symbol.

4. Freedom and Sanctity

Saint Augustine distinguishes two different kinds of freedom. One of them is *liberum arbitrium*, the power of choice in the will. This freedom is an either/or: either you have it, or you don't. All human beings have it at all times, even when its exercise is prevented by sleep, drugs, or infancy in body or mind. The other kind of freedom Augustine calls *libertas*, or liberty. It is freedom from the addiction that is sin. There are degrees of this. You can be more or less free. The first freedom is a means to the end of the second freedom. Mary is maximally free here because she is at the end: she is the perfect saint.

A saint is essentially a lover (of God and man, the two great commandments), and there is no love without freedom. Our free choice to love God is the one thing God Himself cannot give Himself. Mary's *fiat* is her freely given gift (of her whole self, including her freedom!) to God. She gives it away, and only thus does she perfect it. This is the great paradox of saving yourself by losing yourself to God instead of losing yourself by trying to save yourself by living only from and for yourself. It is the paradox of finding (eternal) life by dying (to yourself) instead of finding (eternal) death by refusing to die to yourself. This "dying to yourself" is not just an exaggerated way of speaking about merely altruism and philanthropy and doing good deeds. It is not just ethical but anthropological and even metaphysical. It is anthropological because it is the only way to become a true human self, and it is metaphysical because it is the only way to become really real, solid, thick, authentic, true. The alternative is not only wicked (ethically) but inhuman (anthropologically) and ghostly (metaphysically).

When Eve said her "No" to God, she became not only

less good but also less human and less real. When Mary "reversed the curse" with her "Yes" (*fiat*), she affirmed and fulfilled not only her virtue but also her humanness and her true being. Free will means that we can choose "to be or not to be", to become more real (that is what Heaven is) or less real (that is what Hell is). Her explicit "be" to the fulfillment of God's word and will was also her implicit "be" to the fulfillment of her own being.

5. Seven Kinds of Freedom

If this "big picture" is too profound and not clear enough, let's be a little more clear and less profound. We need to make some distinctions.

The first one we have already noted: Saint Augustine's distinction between the lesser freedom, free will, and the greater freedom, liberty from sin.

In addition to these two, there are least five other meanings to the word "freedom". This makes at least seven possible meanings to this often misunderstood concept.

First, there is physical freedom to act, to walk, talk, see, etc. This is taken away by paralysis, blindness, etc., either by nature or by man (imprisoning, chaining, blinding, etc.). It is limited by many things but totally taken away only by death. This "freedom" is almost the same as "power". Yet although everyone quotes Burke's saying that "all power tends to corrupt, and absolute power corrupts absolutely", yet no one says that about freedom. Yet it is clear to everyone except the most naïve that if we had no limits to our physical freedom, we would become hopelessly corrupted and miserable by our unlimited powers. If you do not believe that, see the Jim Carrey movie *Bruce Almighty*.

Second, there is economic freedom, both personal (having private property) and social (having a "free market" economy). This is the freedom to get or buy or use or control physical things. This also can be taken away either by nature, in poverty, or by man, in communism or any other totalitarianism.

Third, there is the freedom to be the master of your own life. This is the freedom that is taken away by slavery, when you are owned and controlled by another and reduced to a piece of property.

Fourth, there is political freedom, which is taken away by tyranny, in various degrees.

Fifth, there is emotional or psychological freedom, freedom from misery and depression, anxiety and fear. This can be addressed, and raised or lowered, by drugs or psychotherapy as well as by a variety of distractions such as winning the lottery. Its most effective treatment is faith, hope, and love, the three medicines for the soul provided by the Great Physician.

Sixth, there is freedom from sin (*libertas*), which is bestowed only by God. Since all sin is against God, it can be forgiven only by God (justification) and eliminated only by God ("sanctification"). Both require our free cooperation, i.e., the seventh kind of freedom.

This seventh kind of freedom, or free will, is freedom from determinism, and this freedom is taken away by no one, not even God. This freedom is the necessary condition or presupposition of all morality. Robots and rocks and lilies and lions have no morality because they have no free choice. If free will does not exist, all moral language is meaningless: praising, blaming, rewarding, punishing, counseling, and commanding. We do not do these things to machines, even to our most complicated computers.

Typically, modern man acknowledges and seeks the first five freedoms, but not the sixth one, and sometimes he even denies the seventh.

Which of these seven freedoms did Mary have?

(1) She had the physical freedom that nearly all of us have, of course. But she did not misuse it, as we all sometimes do.

(2) She had some economic freedom, but not much, both because she was poor and because under the Roman yoke taxation was oppressive and unjust.

(3) She was not anyone's slave. She was not "owned" by another human being. Of course she was "owned" by God, but that made her maximally free, not enslaved, because God is love and God is truth. Love and truth are the only two things that always set you free.

(4) She had very little political freedom under Roman despotism. But that was surprisingly unimportant to her destiny, to her sanctity, and to the meaning of her life.

(5) She had great psychological freedom even though she had exceedingly great sorrows. This also shows us something surprising: that holiness is the very best psychotherapy.

(6) She had total freedom from sin, both original and actual.

(7) And she had the same free will, or free choice, that we all have.

The highest freedom is sanctity, freedom from sin (for all sin is addiction). Mary is maximally free because she is maximally holy. Compared with this, all the other freedoms almost fade to nothing in importance.

The reason for the close connection between freedom and sanctity is that the essence of sanctity is obedience to the two great commandments of love, and love and freedom go together. The more we love, the more free we become from the master addiction, selfishness, which is the essence of sin. So freedom is both the origin and the end of love: free will is love's origin, and liberty is love's end.

Mary's *fiat* is the freely given gift of her very freedom to God. She perfects her freedom by giving it away. This reveals to us how close to the very essence of the self freedom is, for the self is also something that we can perfect and keep only by giving it away—see John 12:25, the great mystery that every authentic religion has discovered. This mystery, and paradox, is the deepest, most profound, and most important discovery in all of anthropology. The whole purpose, design, end, goal, fulfillment, success, flourishing, joy, and happiness of the self is in freely giving itself away. Mary alone fulfills that teleology perfectly in this world. She is "our tainted nature's solitary boast".

This anthropological principle has metaphysical consequences. The holier you are, the realer you are. This is strikingly clear in Dante, and in C. S. Lewis' delightful little abbreviation and updating of Dante in *The Great Divorce*.

6. Freedom and the Body

There is a surprise when we analyze just where Mary's free will resides. Of course, it is first of all in the soul; in fact, the body, *by itself*, is not free. But insofar as the soul is free, the body is, too. For the body is not just matter but the matter *of the soul* as the soul is "the form of the body".

Mary's free will is shown most clearly in her *fiat* at the Annunciation. Saint John Paul II writes, in *Mulieris Dignitatem*: "All of God's action in human history at all times respects the free will of the human 'I.' And such was the case with

the Annunciation at Nazareth." He speaks of Mary's free
will at the Annunciation in a way that we find surprising
because it is not purely "spiritual" or a matter of the soul
alone, and not purely physical, either, but whole-person-
al: "Through her response of faith Mary exercises her free
will. . . . By responding with her '*fiat*', Mary . . . *is truly the
Mother of God, because motherhood concerns the whole person*, not
just the body." Joseph Ratzinger, in "Mariology and Marian
Spirituality", says: "It is precisely as a woman that she exemplifies saved and liberated mankind. . . . The 'biological'
is inseparable from the human, just as the human is inseparable from the 'theological'." No Cartesian dualism here.
The entity in which free will abides is the whole person,
the "I". The same is true of motherhood. It is not purely
biological or purely spiritual and not two different things
related only extrinsically by efficient causality or even only
by final causality. It is related intrinsically by material and
formal causality. It is "bio-spiritual".

Mary's self and her freedom are not just in her soul but
also in her body, since it is in the one "I" or person that is
both soul and body. But, of course, it is first of all in her
soul, and it is primarily in her soul. Her Magnificat shows
this, when she says that it is her soul that magnifies the Lord
and it is her spirit that rejoices in God her Savior. She is
not a body with a soul but a soul with a body. The body
does not have the power to say "I". But it has the power
to incarnate it. The soul has the power to choose and to
command the act, but the act of procreation is a bodily act.
It is one of the many things an angel cannot do—perhaps
the most powerful and holy of all those things an angel cannot do. Angels may have been instrumental causes of God's
act of creation, and they probably helped and continue to
help it to flourish, as water does to plants; but they cannot

be even instrumental causes of an eternal soul, as we can. Angels cannot procreate.

God Himself, in Mary's womb, became an embodied God, embodied in a human nature that is both body and soul. That soul has human feelings, emotions, sorrows, and limits, including mortality, none of which God had before. And He still has all this, for the Ascension was not the undoing of the Incarnation.

~

How are the soul and body related? One of the best answers to that question is that soul and body image each other. We all know that bodies image souls. But the imaging works the other way around, too. Wittgenstein, asked by skeptical materialistic philosopher friends what the "soul" looked like, replied, "Like the body". A picture (a photo, a portrait, or a bust) looks like a person, but we also say of a person "You look just like your picture."

We are not surprised by bodies imaging souls, but we are surprised by souls imaging bodies; and that tells us how Cartesian, how dualistic, our thinking still is, despite the Incarnation. We are surprised by Wittgenstein's saying. But we are not surprised by the cliché that "the eyes are the windows of the soul." Even preverbal babies implicitly know that bodies image and manifest souls, for they know that smiles express happiness and frowns express the opposite. Only the "experts" are able to ignore that. For instance, the experts in the Global Happiness Project rated the five Scandinavian countries the happiest on earth and five nations in sub-Saharan Africa the unhappiest. Of course. We always speak of "those dour Africans" and "those smiling

Scandinavians" and of the wonderfully low suicide rate in Scandinavia and the high suicide rate in Africa. Not! What could possibly cause such idiocy? It is simple. "Experts" want to be scientific, and science seeks quantification, and you can quantify bank accounts but not happiness. This is what happens when the STEM courses displace and eliminate the Humanities.

Ask yourself: Would Mary feel more at home in Scandinavia or in Africa? Is there more devotion to her and to motherhood in Scandinavia or in Africa? Where is bodily life more sacred? Where do people still believe souls even exist? Where are both virginity and procreation respected more?

The modern world has managed to combine two opposite errors in its philosophy of human nature: materialism and spiritualism. The refutation of materialism is: "My soul magnifies the Lord and my spirit rejoices in His salvation." The refutation of spiritualism is procreation. The Magnificat and the Nativity refute our two leading anthropological heresies.

The perfect example of the body imaging the soul, and the practical, moral consequence of it, is the line from the Tysk hymn celebrating Mary's virginity and motherhood, both of which express in the body the same thing in the soul: giving up her whole self to God: "Let my soul, like Mary, / Be Thine earthly sanctuary."

7. *Sex and Divine Design*

In a God-designed universe, nothing is random; everything is teleological, designed for a purpose. What is the divinely designed purpose of the body and its sexuality?

Most generally, to express the soul. More particularly, to

procreate new souls and bodies. Human procreation images divine creation. For the image of God is in the body as well as the soul (see Gen 1:27).

There are at least three natural, intrinsic ends or purposes in the divine design of sexual intercourse: procreation, personal union, and pleasure. Of these three ends, the first is the most obvious, the most important (if the human race is to continue), and the most high and holy, since its product is literally without price: a person, the only thing in the universe that has value for his own sake, not merely as a means to another end, and the only thing capable of hypostatic and ecstatic union with God. The other two ends, the union between two persons in both body and soul and intense pleasure and joy, exist for those persons, not as ends in themselves. They are (in the language of philosophy) "accidental" rather than "essential", though they are "proper accidents". They are not substantial; they exist, not in or for themselves, but only in and for persons.

Sex is holy because its product, human life, is holy—life as such, life as a whole, all life. As Chesterton said, paganism was optimistic about many little things but pessimistic about Everything, about the one big thing, about Everything, about the meaning of it all. Christianity is the opposite: no matter how pessimistic one may have to be about little things like pain and poverty and suffering and even martyrdom, it is optimistic (or rather full of hope) about Everything. "One thing is needful: Everything. The rest is vanity of vanities" (Chesterton). Paganism did not see holiness in sex because sex is the origin of life and paganism did not see holiness in life. For pagans, life led only to death, or at best to a vague, ghostlike existence in a dark underworld, not to eternal light and joy and union with God. Paganism is bad news; Christianity is "good news".

Paganism returned when Christendom became "Western Civilization", or apostate Christendom. Sex's purpose is now pleasure or union but not procreation. In fact its deliberate purpose is usually *avoiding* procreation. We say "Blessed are the barren", blessed are those whose contraceptives work. In fact, the whole purpose of contraception is to be as totally opposite as possible to the Virgin Mother: to be a non-virginal non-mother.

8. Femininity

Man (mankind, the species, *Anthropos, homo*) is heterosexual. That is simply a biological fact, however much that fact is hated, denied, feared, ignored, bent, mutilated, altered, ideologized, relativized, or subjectivized by a small group of influential people (the mind-molders, "the chattering classes") in a small area of the world (Europe and North America) in a small chunk of time (the last generation or two).

If the species is heterosexual, a complete philosophy of man (*Anthropos*, the species) must include a philosophy not only of man (*vir*) but also of woman (*mulier*).

Jesus is the perfect man, and Mary is the perfect woman.

What is a woman?

The first and most obvious answer is that a woman is or can be a mother. A man cannot.

"Mother"—it is the word dying soldiers often say at the hour of their death. Death is one of the two most important times in our life, the other being now. Eternity touches time only in those two moments. That is why we ask Mary to "pray for us sinners now and at the hour of our death." The "Hail Mary" wastes no words or times.

Mary is the mother of . . . whom? Of God, first of all,

for she is the mother of Jesus, and Jesus is God. It is a syllogism, and Protestants can protest against the title in the conclusion of that syllogism only by denying one of its two premises.

Second, from the Cross, Jesus gave her to John and John to her; and John stands for all faithful Christians, since he was the only one of the disciples, except the women, who remained faithful to Him to the end; therefore, she is the mother of all disciples, all Christians.

Third, she is the Mother of the Church, because if we are John's disciples, then we are Jesus' disciples, and if we are Jesus' disciples, then we are the Church, "the people of God" and "the Mystical Body of Christ".

~

Mary shows us what a woman is, i.e., what womanhood, or femininity, is. The next few pages will help us to understand and appreciate Mary even though they do not mention her name because they are about what she is, which is a perfect woman.

There are three logically possible philosophies of womanhood and manhood: one underestimates their oneness, one underestimates their twoness, and one underestimates neither.

The underestimation of their oneness sees men and women as two species destined to misunderstand each other forever. "Men are from Mars; Women are from Venus." So-called "feminists" who hold this nowadays often speak of "toxic" masculinity.

The underestimation of their twoness is the currently fashionable unisexism. It involves a knee-jerk reaction against the very word "femininity", the very concept of a woman's essential "nature", or that of a man. Thus gender fluidity, "gender bending", and the deliberate "transgressivism" of transgenderism, which is based on the astonishing, and astonishingly popular, lie that "you can be whatever you want to be." Thus, the law decreeing that there are not two but fifty-two different genders in Canada. (Stay tuned for larger numbers tomorrow.) Thus, Harvard's firing of President Larry Summers for daring to suggest that the traditional idea be allowed even to be discussed.

The third and only sane and happy alternative is complementarity, or *vive la différence*. Here, masculinity and femininity are related like yang and yin, right and left, sun and moon, day and night, words and music, head and heart, bacon and eggs, land and sea. This view sees an analogy between spirit and matter, man and nature, so that the body reflects the spirit: phallus and womb, exteriority and interiority. Thus, there is inter-dependence, inter-fulfillment, inter-course, inter-action, inter-parenting, inter-learning (from each other), and inter-admiration and superiority. This allows both parties to experience admiration for the other and gives both the privilege of experiencing two great joys and practicing two great virtues: the joy of admiration and the virtue of humility on the part of the inferior or admirer, and the joy of service and the virtue of magnanimity and generosity on the part of the superior. For each is both superior and inferior to the other.

It is only ideology, not empirical science, experience, or ecumenical, cross-cultural, nearly universal common sense, that denies the fact that men and women are different.

The difference is not total, either like light vs. darkness or like two vs. three, but relative, like high vs. low, dark vs. light, or quick vs. slow.

It is also physical as well as spiritual: men's voices tend to be lower and women's higher because of vocal cord structure; and women have more endurance, both short- and long-range, while men have more upper body strength. Whether one is a materialist and looks only at genetic structures, brain functions, and empirical actions, or whether one is a spiritualist and looks only at thoughts and feelings and choices, or whether one is a dualist and looks at these two things as if they were independent, or whether one is a commonsense Aristotelian hylomorphist who sees body and soul, or body and mind, as two equally real dimensions, we find the same differences between men and women.

But both physically and spiritually, these are tendencies, not absolutes, or (to use another analogy) partly overlapping features. For instance, men have a little estrogen, and women have a little testosterone. The fifty-one structural and functional differences between the male and female human brains are all matters of more or less, faster or slower, rather than either/or. The only exception is the biological fact that men do not have vaginas and wombs and women do not have penises.

We all know what the nonphysical differences are.

First, men tend to value and use reason more, while women tend to value and use instinct more. Saint John Paul II, in *Mulieris Dignitatem*, said that there is "that 'genius' which belongs to women and which can ensure sensitivity for human beings in every circumstance." Saint Edith Stein wrote: "Mary at the wedding at Cana in her quiet, observing look surveys everything and discovers what is lacking. Before anything is noticed, even before embarrassment sets in, she has procured already the remedy. She finds ways and means, she gives necessary directives, doing all quietly. She draws no attention to herself. Let her be the prototype of woman in professional life." Saint Edith calls this the "ethos" of woman: "*an inner form*, a constant *spiritual attitude*" toward other persons. "Woman naturally seeks to embrace that which is *living, personal, and whole*" (*Essays on Woman*).

Second, men's primary value tends to be truth, including moral truth, especially the truth that takes the form of justice, while women's primary value tends to be love, especially the love that takes the form of mercy and compassion.

Here is an example that may seem extreme to men but not to women. Saint Gemma Galgani was praying to Christ for the soul of a notorious sinner, and Christ listed to her the sinner's terrible sins and three times refused to give him the grace of repentance. The saint then said: "If you refuse, I shall ask Your mother." Christ replied: "In that case, I cannot refuse." That same day the sinner came to Confession.

Of course, Christ from the beginning had planned that, as He had planned His mother's role in the wedding feast at Cana. You cannot change God's mind and will. But you can fulfill it by appealing to mercy, which is changeable, as well as by appealing to justice, which is unchangeable.

Third, men tend to individualism and an assertion of their rights and freedoms, while women tend to be more relational or communal and respond to needs.

Fourth, men tend to suppress nonviolent emotions, while women tend to express them more, while the opposite is true of violent emotions. The vast majority of violent crimes are committed by men. Men also tend to talk less, the more emotional they become, while women tend to talk more. (This is connected with the fact that there are more connections, in both structure and function, in the female brain between the hemisphere that controls speech and the hemisphere that controls emotion.)

Fifth, men tend to competition (thus, they are more "into" wars, sports, and competitive games), while women tend to collaboration.

Sixth, men tend to appeal to impersonal principles, while women tend to appeal to persons. Thus, it is a man who writes to his beloved: "I could not love thee, dear, so much/ Loved I not honor more."

Seventh, men tend to absolutism, and women to compromise.

Eighth, men's typical psychological problem is having too much ego and self-esteem, while women's typical psychological problem is having too little.

Ninth, men tend to emphasize doing, while women emphasize being. Men have no wombs and forge their identities in the outside world by their actions and achievements. Women have a built-in identity and vocation in their bodies. As Mister Rogers put it, "Boys are fancy on the outside, girls are fancy on the inside. Everybody's fancy, everybody's fine; your body's fancy and so is mine."

This is not the only list. We could add many more features or add more distinctions within these ten. We could also condense the number by showing connections.

Mary here is typical of a woman. This is part of her perfection, for God designed women to be all of these things, as part of human nature. That nature is fallen and broken, but a broken stick is still a stick, not a stone.

We can see Mary's femininity in each of the few passages in Scripture about her. For instance, as Saint Edith Stein said, Mary's intuition is seen by the fact that it is she who at Cana intuitively notices the failing of the wine and the embarrassment of the host. And Mary's communalism and relational nature is shown by the Visitation: immediately after the Annunciation, Mary immediately shares her unique grace with her cousin. Also, she and two other Marys stay with Christ at the Cross, while eleven of the twelve apostles run away.

9. Mary and Feminism

To speak of "Mary and feminism" is like speaking about "the apostles and Judas Iscariot" or "democracy and the People's Republic of China".

Mary is the true feminist, and therefore many modern "feminists" despise her Catholic image, thinking of her as a fearful, passive, weak, conformist, superstitious, oppressed slave to a male chauvinist society. Yet she is the most powerful merely human being who ever lived, and Satan fears her more than all the angels. She is the dragon-slayer, and Satan is the dragon crushed under her feet. (Look at the icon of Our Lady of Guadalupe.) She does to Satan what Judith did to Holofernes. (Read the Book of Judith; great story!) She is no pacifist. She is a warrior. But she understands that our enemy is spiritual (Eph 6:12), and her weapons are spiritual: humility, obedience, surrender, and love. (These are *weapons*! Did you know that? Did you know that we are at war?)

Mary is not a patsy, a sissy, a doormat, a decoration, or a softie! She is tough! She is a warrior! A woman is not "a soft man". (That is the classic male chauvinist definition of a woman.) Nor is a man a hard woman. That is not the definition of a man or of a woman but of a "feminist". (Cue in the canned laughter now.)

A test of true feminism is one's reaction to the most common of all icons, that of the Madonna and Child. Put such an icon in front of some modern "feminists", and it is like putting a crucifix in front of a vampire. To call these people "feminists" is like calling cannibals "chefs". But our propaganda has validated Hitler's theory about the "Big Lie". In our linguistically corrupted society, sodomy is called marriage, men are called wives, boys are called girls, paralyzed human beings are called vegetables, children are called accidents, those who kill children in the womb are called doctors, physicians, or healers, pregnancy is treated as a disease, and telling the truth out of love is called hate speech.

The dignity of woman, and of Mary as the ideal woman, is clear in Scripture. Christ did not undermine her dignity by calling her "woman" at Cana (Jn 2:4) or at Calvary (Jn 19:26). It was a word of honor rather than dishonor because it bestowed on her a universal and archetypal status, as it did on Eve, who was called simply "the woman" throughout the story of the Fall in Genesis 3. Christ also used that name at Cana, when Mary implicitly asked Him to change His plans and to begin His public ministry now by performing His first public miracle. He replied, "Woman, what have you to do with me? My hour has not yet come." This sounds like a rebuke, but it was not. Christ was addressing her here as the archetype, the New Eve, and Mary was consenting to lose Him as her son to His vocation to martyrdom. She was doing at Cana the same thing she did at the Presentation in the Temple: offering her precious child up to God to be used—in fact, killed, oblated, sacrificed—for our salvation. The Presentation in the Temple was in a way the first Mass. And at Cana, she repeated this offering.

In Genesis, Eve is not called "Eve" but "the woman" because she is not just an individual but the whole human race, for she was literally the mother of all the living. We have four universal archetypes here: Mary was the Second Eve as Christ was the Second Adam (Rom 5), and Christ makes all things new (Rev 21:5), including not only man but also woman. Mary becomes spiritually the new mother of all the living, i.e., all those who have in their souls eternal life, the life of her Son. As Adam was not just an individual (he was that, too), but Mankind; and as Eve was not just an individual (she was that, too), but Womankind, so as Christ was the New Adam in both senses, so Mary is the New Eve in both senses.

We understand any living thing—plant, animal, person —best in its maturity, its consummation, its perfection. We understand the perfection of man best in Jesus and the perfection of woman best in Mary. Both Jesus and Mary are archetypes for both genders, for both exemplify the perfection of "the image of God" in human nature, and that image is "male *and* female" (Gen 1:27), whether that perfect human nature is joined to the divine nature, as it is in Christ, or whether it is simply human, as it is in Mary. So Christ is relevant to women as well as to men, and Mary is relevant to men as well as to women.

10. Marian Eschatological Anthropology

Aristotle wisely and commonsensically observed that we can understand the essential nature of anything best from considering it in its maturity and perfection. We understand the acorn from the oak better than vice versa. Apply this to anthropology, and the conclusion emerges that the fullest understanding of human nature is to be found in its ultimate end, purpose, destiny, and design. This is twofold: before and after death. The before-death perfection is relative to the after-death perfection, so anthropology is relative to eschatology. Life in this universe is like life in the womb (unless the basic hope and conviction of nearly all religions and nearly all mankind is a hoax and death ends everything). This universe is a large womb, and, as we understand a fetus best (and also an infant and a teenager) by understanding a mature adult human being, so we understand what we are now best by understanding what we will be eternally.

This principle is true even if what we understand about our postmortem identity is very obscure and thin. Which, of course, it is. But it is not nonexistent. We have clues, like roads pointing in a certain direction. And we have analogies. I just used one of them: the adult in this world is to the saint in the next life as the fetus is to the adult, and this universe is to Heaven as a womb is to this universe.

What clues or analogies do we have, then, and what does Mary have to do with it?

Our primary clue is Christ, since He reveals not only God most clearly to us but also ourselves.

Christopher Derrick wrote a striking and thoughtful short poem about what may be called Christ's eschatological anthropology, and I have written a longer commentary on what could be called Mary's role in that.

"The Resurrection of the Body"
by Christopher Derrick

He's a terror, that one:
Turns water into wine,
Wine into blood—
I wonder what He turns blood into?

"Maria Eucharistica"
by Peter Kreeft

At Cana, she observed: "They have no wine."
Not a command,
Not even a request,
Just a fact.
But freighted heavily with a woman's implications:
"I know You.
I know Your compassion.
I know You will do something Christlike."

"But my hour is not yet come."

No answer, in words, but the silent Mona Lisa smile
    was enough.

So He "did it again":
As He had made rain fall on the grapevine each year,
Turning water into wine in the transformation factory of
    Mother Earth
(for although miracles are not natural, nature is miraculous),
He now, for her, speeded up the process
And invited His guests to drink from the cup of His
    wine-making rain.

Three years later, in the Upper Room, He "did it again":
He took the wine He had made out of water
And made it into blood—His blood.

It was not Joseph's blood; it was Mary's blood.
Every drop of His blood He got from her,
And all of His body.
Body of Christ, from Mary's body;
Blood of Christ, from Mary's blood.

He had done this before, too, in the transformation
  factory of the human body,
Which turned the wine drunk at every meal into blood.
But now, for us, His guests, He speeded up the process
And invited us to drink from the cup of His veins.

He will "do it again" in the Resurrection,
When He takes our blood, the life of our body, and
  transforms it again
Into something that eye has not seen, nor ear heard,
  nor has it entered into the heart of man.

In what transformation factory?
Who knows?
But I suspect that Mary's name will be on its gates.

Chapter VIII

MARY'S PSYCHOLOGY

Psychology is usually classified under anthropology; but I want to distinguish psychology from anthropology here by three things. First, it is about the psyche, which is only half of us—it is not the body. Second, it is personal (individual) rather than archetypal (universal). Third, it is more practical than theoretical. Psychology and anthropology are not always distinguished in that way, but I trust you will see the reasons for my distinction when you compare this section with the previous one.

1. The Essential Practical Principle of Mary's Psychology

(1) The first absolutely necessary assumption is that man is teleological: purposed, designed, end-oriented. This is simply an observable fact, not an ideology or a faith. It is a truth noted by all cultures and sages except those in modern Western civilization who take physical science as the only valid knowledge. The strictly scientific method cannot measure purpose or design, which is neither visible to the eye nor quantifiable by the computer. This principle of "intelligent design" or teleology is not unique to Mary or Jews or Christians.

(2) The teleological end, as revealed most clearly by Mary's Assumption, is life with God in Heaven. Our origin and design are also our end and destiny, or at least our hope. Some vague and confused version of this hope is also universal among mankind. Hope is as innate and universal to the human psyche as faith.

(3) Between design and destiny comes desire. This is the law of the three D's. Because of our divine design, our desiring hearts are restless until they rest in their destiny. This law, too, is universal; that is why the single most popular Christian book in the world is Augustine's *Confessions* and why that quotation ("Thou hast made us for Thyself, and [therefore] our hearts are restless till they rest in Thee") is the most quoted sentence in all of Christian literature outside the Bible.

(4) Our happiness (*eudaimonia*) is the objectively real and lasting state (*ia*) of having a soul (*daimon*) that is good (*eu*) both mentally (wisdom) and morally (virtue). When Aristotle wrote this word, he was only uttering common sense.

(5) Christians know more than this common sense, but not less. They know that this happiness comes from three things: reflection on our design and our Designer, God our Father and Creator; willing cooperation with His Holy Spirit in our hearts by the active pursuit (choice) and desire (love) for Him and His will (which is the essence of sanctity); and the hope of Heaven and salvation. These three moments of time—past and present and future—are associated especially (though never exclusively) with the three Persons of the Trinity—the Father and the Holy Spirit and the Son—and with the three greatest virtues, faith and charity and hope, respectively.

(6) That is the objective description of our happiness. The subjective description of it is that it exists on three lev-

els: pleasure (in the body), satisfaction or peace or contentment (in the heart and soul), and joy (in the spirit).

(7) The First Cause of this happiness is God. He is its
formal cause, its form or shape or quality or nature, which
is *agape* love. He is a Trinity of Lover, Beloved, and Loving
because that is complete love and that is His very essence
and life: perfect, total, infinite, and eternal self-giving Love.
That is what God is as the "formal cause" or nature of our
happiness.

He is also the "material cause" (in the Aristotelian sense)
of our happiness in that real union with him is that out of
which our happiness is made, that in which it consists.

He is also its final cause, what our happiness is "about"
or "toward". Happiness without Him would be like words
without meaning or arrows without a target.

And He is its efficient cause, too, because we cannot give
it (true, total, adequate, final, immortal happiness) to ourselves; He must give it to us as His gift, His grace.

(8) Therefore, our practical road to joy is our faith and
hope and love of Him, our *islam* (surrender, submission) to
Him. This is the essence of holiness, which is the secret of
happiness.

No one ever showed this more clearly and more perfectly
than Mary (see Lk 1:48).

2. The Problem of Evil:
Resistance or Nonresistance?

Obviously the answer to that question depends on the kind
of evil. Moral evil is always to be resisted; physical evil,
suffering, physical or emotional, is sometimes to be fought
and sometimes to be endured. That double attitude is clear.

But when? When are we to accept suffering as God's will, and when are we to fight against it, in ourselves as well as in others, as much as we can? Can we do both?

The obviously most prominent problem for practical psychology is human unhappiness or suffering. The theoretical, or philosophical, "problem of evil" (the fact that evil exists even though an infinitely good and powerful God also exists) has been dealt with above. But what about the practical psychological problem?

Mary knew from personal experience the greatest of evils in sharing and participating in the Passion and death of her Son. This was the greatest moral evil ever committed—the torture and murder of God—and also the greatest physical suffering the world that the Devil could invent. It was also, on Christ's part, the greatest emotional suffering, because He must have known that despite all that He did, some of His infinitely beloved children would reject Him and be lost forever. (This was probably the temptation the Devil showed him in Gethsemane.) How did Mary deal with this horrendous suffering, especially in light of her faith in the perfect God with a perfect will?

To answer this question completely, we must distinguish between God's revealed will and His hidden will. God does not have two wills, but His will appears to us in two different ways. Some of it is hidden, and some of it is revealed.

His clearly revealed will, His law, is our way to happiness. But much of His will is hidden, including how He deals with sin and its effects. His revealed will is a "No" to all evil, but His hidden will is a Providential permitting and a using of evil, including not only suffering (physical evil) but also even sin (moral evil), together with some of the effects of sin, namely, the sufferings it brings, for the end of a greater good for us in the end. This good happens at two times, both in the present (the preservation of our free will in the case of sin and our training in wisdom, courage, and faith by suffering) and in the future, for our greatest joy in the end.

Since His will appears to us in two different ways, our attitude toward it should also be twofold. We are to fight sin without qualification, by supernatural faith, hope, and love, and we are to fight pain with qualification, both in ourselves, by our natural, God-designed instincts, and in others, by our compassion, which is also a natural instinct ("the herd instinct") as well as a cultivated moral virtue. God looks approvingly not only on saints but also on doctors and scientists who invent cures for diseases. But our attitude toward God's hidden will must be faith in the head and the trust in the heart that He is working things out in the best possible way: the Romans 8:28 principle. By nature, we love sin and hate suffering; by grace, we hate sin and endure suffering as God's will for us.

The greatest exemplar of both is Mary, who sinned the least and suffered the most. She accepted both parts of God's will, and, therefore, she both did and did not "resist evil", as Christ paradoxically taught in the Sermon on the Mount. She did not endure sin but resisted it; she did not resist suffering but endured it. She trusted that even the horrible sufferings that came to her and her Son were part of God's perfect plan. And they were.

Without this double attitude, we either accept evils even when we can and should do something about them, or we distrust God's hidden will when confronting the evils we can do nothing about. This double attitude is psychologically similar to "love the sinner, hate the sin." The only two alternatives are unthinkable: to hate sinners or to love sins. The only two alternatives to Mary's double attitude to

God's will are either rebellion at His Law or rebellion at His patience.

3. The Psychology of Freedom and Happiness

There are many varieties of "feminism", but the radical modern "feminists" who make the most news and noise today typically want to be more like men. They prize freedom: from men, from marriage, from children, from family. Mary is free in another, deeper way. She is self-giving, virtuous, heavenly, humble, and at peace. She sees love as freedom's end. She has the properties of what Saint Ignatius Loyola calls "the spirit of consolation". Modern feminists are typically egotistical, lustful, worldly, arrogant, and troubled. They have what Saint Ignatius calls "the spirit of desolation". They see love (Mary's kind of love) as freedom's enemy.

These "feminists" (I put the word in quotes deliberately) typically claim to be "enlightened" and "emancipated". Mary is really emancipated—from that endarkenment.

The psychological opposite of freedom is addiction. Modern "feminists" are typically addicted to their own freedom, to themselves, to their own power. That is the master addiction. They want to "find themselves" and "be themselves". Mary is free because she gives herself away. She does not seek power, and she is the most powerful woman who ever lived.

Mary understands the secret of happiness. It is all in John 12:24–25. It was the quotation Dostoyevsky put at the beginning of *The Brothers Karamazov*, the world's greatest novel. If the brothers had been sisters, Alyosha would be Mary and Ivan would be a modern feminist.

4. Joy and Sorrow

Joy and sorrow are relative to each other, like mountains and valleys. Mary excelled in both. She should be as famous for her joys as for her sorrows.

Her greatest joy was in God. Her whole heart and soul "rejoiced" in God, as she confessed in her Magnificat. But she also experienced the "seven sorrows" of the sword that pierced her to the heart, as Simeon prophesied at the Presentation in the Temple. For she shared Christ's sorrows more totally than anyone else ever did. I cannot imagine any greater sorrow than that of a mother for her suffering child. If this is true for a sinful mother, it is even more true for Mary.

Both her joys and her sorrows came from the same cause: her love. Love always multiplies both joys and sorrows by the multiplier of how much you love. The more you love, the more joy you have. And the more you love, the more sorrows you have.

But what did Simeon mean by saying that the sword of suffering would pierce her heart "that thoughts out of many hearts may be revealed"?

I am not sure, but I suspect that one of the answers to that question is that our attitude toward Mary, especially in her sufferings, like our attitude to Christ and His sufferings, reveals our own deepest heart.

This can be seen, by contrast, with Muhammad, who insisted that Jesus could not have been crucified because he was a prophet and Allah would never allow His prophet to suffer disgrace. I think my very deepest disagreement with Islam is right there. I am a coward when it comes to pain, but I admire the saints who suffer; I am not scandalized by them. To be scandalized by public disgrace is implicitly to put worldly success above fidelity to God. It insists on "success". It admires "winners" and not "losers". It is tempted to use force to "win". Implicitly it sees suffering as the worst of evils. Even pagan Plato knew better than that. In the *Gorgias*, he argues that it is far better to suffer evil than to do it. Socrates, the pagan who perhaps came the closest to the spirit of Christ, suffered public humiliation, disgrace, misunderstanding, and execution, not for his evil, but for his goodness. Implicitly, Muhammad is saying, with Freud, that pain (at least the emotional pain of public failure) is the greatest evil. Buddha also implicitly sees suffering as the greatest evil, for his whole religion is aimed at eliminating suffering. Christianity is radically different: it eliminates sin, and it does so *through* suffering. In fact, it sees God Himself suffering maximally.

Simeon is predicting the suffering of both Mary and Christ; and, like everything about them, this reveals, not just them, but also us. Christ was like a mirror: everyone who ever met him came away with a new knowledge of himself. Mary is the same. Simeon is implicitly predicting what happened in Christ's meeting with Veronica on the *via dolorosa*. Her veil, her cloth that she gave to the suffering Christ to wipe His brow instead of keeping it for her own use and beauty, is a true icon of Himself (that is the literal meaning of her name "Veronica"—*vere eikon*).

Mary's wisdom transcended the shallowness that saw sorrow and suffering as the greatest evil, unlike the "wisdom" of both the materialist Freud and the immaterialist Buddha. She knew something far better than pleasure—the joy that comes from God alone—and therefore, in that light, something far worse than pain: sin, which is separation from that God and from that joy. Mary did not experience sin in her own person, either Original Sin or actual sin, but she experienced its effects in her own person more acutely than anyone else when she was deprived of her Son for three days at age twelve when He was lost and, again, on Good Friday and Holy Saturday, when He was dead. Only someone who knew divine joy as intimately as Mary did could know divine sorrow as intimately as Mary did. Only one so close to Heaven, that is, to Christ, can be so close to Hell, that is, to the loss of Christ. In her *fiat*, Mary was accepting both that highest of all mountaintops and that darkest of all valleys. You can see both if you prayerfully meditate on Michelangelo's masterpiece, the *Pietà*.

~

Mary's wisdom *about* suffering was a wisdom that came *from* suffering. That wisdom is best appreciated by contrast with its lower levels. Here are seven levels of wisdom about suffering:

The lowest level, the most stupid and sinful folly, sees sorrow and pain as the greatest, or even the only, evil and seeks to avoid it by any means. This is pure utilitarianism, the most unethical of all ethics, the most amoral of all "moralities".

The second level simply qualifies the means to avoid pain and attain pleasure. It admits that not everything is morally permissible. But it is as materialistic and hedonistic as the first level about pleasure being the meaning of life; but it is inconsistent enough to listen to moral common sense in admitting moral laws against causing others pain. But pain is still the essential evil.

The third level is the weak wisdom that admits that sin is a greater evil than pain, but only as a concession that does not go very deeply into the heart.

A fourth level, Stoicism, is the firm conviction that spiritual evil is not only the greatest but even the only evil and steels itself to suffering, attempting by detachment to overcome the passions of desire for pleasure and fear of pain, both for oneself and for others. But in this philosophy, pity and compassion are seen as weaknesses. Stoics are not slobs, like hedonists, but tend to be snobs, like Pharisees.

A fifth level is the level of a faith that accepts suffering and sorrow, trusting in God, or something like God, who wills it, but asks that it be removed at the same time as it seeks to endure it. This is the natural double attitude discussed above. This is where most serious Christians are.

A sixth level, common to all the saints, is the will not only to endure suffering as an unfortunate necessity but even the will to suffer actively for the sake of charity to others or reparation to God for His glory. This is a supernatural gift of charity, and it is not confined to the saints.

A seventh level is a special rarity even among the saints: the love that seeks out great suffering for pure charity's sake. This is either a special divine gift or a pathological and dangerous self-delusion, and we must resist the temptation to classify all examples of it as either one or the other, since both kinds exist, and Satan apes even the highest things by the lowest and most perverse imitations of them.

Mary's wisdom accepted Simeon's prophecy of the sword that shall pierce her soul because she knew that sword, not as an impersonal force, but as a Divine Person whose essence is love. She had consented to give Him birth forty days and nine months earlier. Her sorrow was destined increasingly to become one with His and was therefore destined to surpass all human sorrow. Even on a human level, it was unsurpassed, for umbilical cords cannot be cut spiritually, only physically.

Fulton Sheen, in *The World's First Love*, says that Mary, on the *via dolorosa*, had to "tread the streets over her own Son's blood. His wounds bled; hers did not. Mothers, seeing their sons suffer, wish it could be their own blood instead of their sons' that is shed. In her case, it was her blood that He shed. Every crimson drop of that blood, every cell of that flesh, she had given to Him."

5. Jesus, Mary, and the Eucharist: Connecting Threads

Christ hides (*vere latitat*) in Mary's womb, as the apotheosis of His (and her) humility. He also hides in the Eucharist, and in the Church, which is a large Eucharist and a large Mary. All its children are hers as well as His.

It may (or perhaps it may not) be appropriate at this point to include a poem about this connection:

"Jesus and Mary" (a Communion hymn)

CHORUS:

Body of Christ, from Mary's body/
Blood of Christ, from Mary's blood
Thanks be to her who gave us Jesus/
Thanks be to Him Who gives us God.

VERSES:

Jesus the Bread, Mary the yeast/
Mary the kitchen, Jesus the Feast
Jesus the Tree of Life, Mary the sod/
Mary our God-bearer, Jesus our God
Mary the soul, Jesus the Vine/
Mary the wine-maker, Jesus the Wine

Mary the silkworm, Jesus the Silk/
Mary our mother's breast, Jesus our Milk
Mary the stem, Jesus the Flower/
Mary the stairway, Jesus the Tower
Mary the boatyard, Jesus the Barque/
Mary our Noah, Jesus our Ark
Mary God's ink, Jesus God's Name/
Mary the burning bush, Jesus the Flame
Mary God's paper, Jesus God's Word/
Mary the nest, Jesus the Bird
Mary the artery, Jesus the Blood/
Mary the floodgate, Jesus the Flood
Mary and Jesus, our castle entire/
Mary the fireplace, Jesus the fire
Mary and Jesus, our riches untold/
Mary the gold mine, Jesus the gold

Chapter IX

MARY'S ETHICS

1. The Three Most Important Words in Ethics

"Ethics" and "morality" are two terms that refer to the same thing but from different points of view. "Ethics" suggests a more objective and universal dimension of it, while "morality" suggests a more subjective and personal dimension of it. In our current culture, "morality" often means simply sexual morality, while ethics means everything else. That is a new meaning of the terms that is unjustified because it is implicit rather than explicit.

Ethics has three fundamental terms, each of which has a starting point, or undefined assumption, like the number one in arithmetic. They cannot be defined in terms that are any more fundamental. They are "good", "right", and "ought", or duty. Many philosophers of language, such as G. E. Moore and Ludwig Wittgenstein, say that they cannot be defined (or at least that the term "good" cannot be defined) in any more fundamental terms.

"Good" connotes an end or goal or value. "Right" (not "rights" like "human rights" or "animal rights", but "right" in the singular) connotes truth about the value or disvalue of human acts or laws that define what acts should be done or avoided. "Ought" or "duty" connotes our experience of being under moral obligation.

The opposite of "good" is "evil" or "bad". The opposite

213

of "right" is "wrong". The opposite of "ought" is "ought not".

The three terms are like doors in a house. The house is ethics, or morality. You can enter the whole house through any one of these three doors. Premodern thinkers usually chose "good", early modern thinkers like Hobbes and Locke chose "right"; and Kant made famous the third starting point of duty or obligation.

The three terms are relative to each other. What is good? To do what is right, which is your duty. What is right? To do good and be good; that is your moral duty. What is duty? To obey the moral law that defines what is right and what is good.

Just as, in speculative (theoretical) philosophy, we can begin with metaphysics (which is about what is real) and then go to epistemology (which is about how we know what is real) or vice versa, so in ethics we can begin with any of these three basic concepts and derive the other two from it.

So we will look at Mary's ethics from these three points of view: the good in sections 2–5, the right in section 6, and the ought in section 7.

2. *Mary's Philosophy of the Good*

Traditional ethics, in defining the good, that is, the ethical good for us, addressed three questions. Most contemporary ethics usually addresses only one.

The three questions can best be remembered by an image from C. S. Lewis' *Mere Christianity*. Ethics is like a set of sailing orders for a fleet of ships, which needs to know the answers to three questions: how the ships are to cooperate, how each is to stay shipshape, and what the mission of the fleet is. Modern ethics usually focuses on the first question, how the ships are to cooperate and not get in each other's way. That is social ethics, how we should treat each other. But in order for that to happen, each ship has to be itself shipshape and healthy and not sink; and that corresponds to individual ethics, moral character, personal virtues versus vices. Modern ethics only sometimes treats that. And the most important question of all is the one modern ethical philosophy almost never treats: What is the mission of the fleet in the first place? Why are they at sea? Is it a naval battle or a cruise? Are they merchant ships or ferries? What is their purpose? That is the question of the "meaning of life", or the purpose of life, or the "greatest good", the *summum bonum*.

To all pre-modern philosophers, that was the first and most important question; to the modern mind, that is the last one we dare ask. And the reason for that reluctance is obvious. It is that all the religions of the world claim to be the answer to that question, and we are terrified of religious disagreement and religious wars and even of hurting anyone's feelings by disagreeing and being "judgmental". We have extended the idea of the separation of church and state to mean the separation of religion from any public discussion at all. We have become as embarrassed about religion as the Victorian English were about sex.

Though he was an atheist, Camus saw the folly of ignoring this question. He famously wrote that the only serious question in philosophy is the question of suicide. "Why do you not kill yourself?" The question amounts to "What is the meaning of life for you?" The "existentialists" are the only school of modern philosophy that dares to raise that question. That is why they are the only interesting school of modern philosophy.

Perhaps another, more hidden reason why we avoid that question is our hedonism and comfort-mongering. Everyone knows that only the wise can answer such a question, and everyone knows that only those who suffer can be wise. But our only attitude toward suffering is to avoid it and usually to avoid even the distressing discussion of it. For the question of suffering and death and evil is a question that all the religions of the world claim to answer.

A third reason we do not raise the question of life's meaning—not just what it is but whether life has any at all—is that we no longer revere motherhood, which is the most concrete and explicit answer to the question for a woman. For the first time in our culture's history, many women no longer think of themselves primarily as birth givers. Why? Because they no longer see life as sacred. If they did, they would long to participate in it in their unique and uniquely powerful way. They often see life as not something worth bringing children into. This is what the prophet Saint John Paul II boldly labelled "the culture of death". In a culture of death, abortion is the real answer to the "problem" of pregnancy for fully one-third of pregnant women, who have not succeeded in contracepting, i.e., preventing the "problem" of pregnancy from taking hold in the first place. Pregnancy, and thus life itself, is treated as a "problem", even as a disease.

A mother who gives birth willingly and wisely exchanges a lesser good for a greater good, exchanges pleasure and convenience for life, endures suffering to conquer death, brings a child into a world in which she knows that he, like her, is doomed to suffer and die—why? Because even this life that is lived in "the valley of the shadow of death" is worth living. That conviction is dying in the West—but not elsewhere in the world. That is why our civilization, which used to be called "Christendom" and which hosted Christ's Church for two thousand years, is being replaced.

Our civilization is not guaranteed survival, only Christ's Church is. And that Church is geographically and culturally mobile. She moved from Jerusalem to Rome, and now she may be moving again, to the global south and east. Soon there will probably be more Christians in Asia than in Europe, more in Latin America than in North America, and more in Africa than on any other continent. Africans typically find our "advanced" attitude toward life literally incomprehensible. They are "primitive"; we are "advanced" —like advanced tooth decay. We are "adult". What does that mean in our culture? Well, ask yourself this question: What is an "adult" movie or an "adult" bookstore? "Adult" means "adulterous". (Soon, I predict, that old-fashioned word will be banned as "judgmental" and "hate speech".)

Mary shows her love of life by giving birth; by her extended family; by her visit to her cousin Elizabeth to celebrate both her and Elizabeth's pregnancy; and by celebrating marriage, wedding, procreation, and children at Cana with feasting and drinking (against all Cathars, Albigensians, Gnostics, Puritans, and "spiritualists"). She is "pro-life" in every way. That is the big picture behind abortion: the question is broader than merely whether it is permissible to murder your own innocent unborn children; the issue is whether life is good in itself and on its own terms or only when your narrow, little, individualistic, autonomous, egotistical, blinkered vision says so.

Everything in Mary's life says that *ens est bonum*, being as such is good. That is her word to us. Her word to us is God's Word to us. She speaks few words because the one Word she "speaks" is all we need. She "speaks" that Word by procreating Him.

3. The Goodness of Procreation

If being as such is good, then human being is especially good. Life is good, in itself. And, therefore, both God's creation of life and our procreation of life are also good in themselves.

We moderns worship "creativity", but not the single most creative thing anyone can ever do (or rather, only a woman can do directly), namely procreation. Its product is not a machine or an idea or a program, but the only thing in the universe that God loves for its own sake absolutely: a person, made in His image, His kid.

Procreation is holy and revelatory of the self-giving nature of God; that is why Satan hates it and attacks it and its product in every way he can. Our culture is increasingly adopting his slogan, "blessed are the barren." The ideal woman from his point of view is the most total anti-Mary: the non-mother, the non-virgin, and the non-saint. Better yet, the anti-mother, anti-virgin, and anti-saint.

There is a close parallel between the two places where God continually performs the most perfect, total, and amazing miracle many times a day: a woman's womb, where God creates new eternal souls, and a Catholic altar, where He transubstantiates bread and wine into the Body and Blood of His Son to give His salvation to His people as concretely and objectively as a garden hose gives water to those who drink from it. That is the deepest reason contraception is not only unnatural but blasphemous: it is deliberately locking the first of those two holy doors to God so that He cannot come in and do His miracle. It is a lie, told not just with the tongue but with the whole body. It is like a priest only pretending to say the words of consecration but not saying them so that God cannot come down on that altar and perform His other great miracle.

In other words, priests do a Mary-like thing in saying the words of consecration.

4. Virtue

From the beginning, Christians saw Mary as holy, as virtuous, as innocent. Even Martin Luther protested against the ignoring or demeaning of Mary that he saw in other Protestants. The Church explained and defined this holiness in the dogma of her Immaculate Conception in 1854. Like all dogmas, the only thing new about it was the formulaic words to define it. The truth that was defined was there, and believed, from the beginning, though not in as explicit a form. Dogmas are like leaves that grow on the tree naturally, from within, not like additional rooms added from without to a man-made building or another stanza to a poem. "Poems are made by fools like me, But only God can make a tree" (Joyce Kilmer).

Virtues are simply good habits. Moral virtues are morally good habits, and vices are morally bad habits. Habits are patterns of acting that are made by repeating the same act again and again. Not only are habits caused by actions, but actions are also caused by habits. The sum of all our moral habits is our moral character. Mary's character was wholly virtuous and innocent. "Immaculate" does not mean merely "virginal" (except to a sex-obsessed culture), it means "free from all vices". By a special grace (she was "*full* of grace", remember: Lk 1:28), she was saved from Original Sin (by the One who saves all of us, including His mother) at her conception, and she never committed any actual sins. The earliest Church Fathers call her "the Second Eve". Like Eve, she was immaculately conceived; like Eve, she had free will; but unlike Eve, she never sinned.

The master virtue is *agape* love, unselfish, self-forgetful, self-sacrificing love, the will to the best good of the other person or persons. When this love meets sufferings and needs, both physical and spiritual, its reaction is compassion (the subjective or emotional dimension) and mercy (the objective aid, beginning with forgiveness rather than judgment). This virtue is to fill all the circles of our life, beginning with our individual relationships, first of all with our parents, then our siblings, then our spouse and children, then our extended family, then our friends, then our tribe or cultural community, then our nation, then our world. Which it indeed did with Mary. For instance, she was at her cousin Elizabeth's house to help with Elizabeth's miraculous old-age pregnancy (the Visitation), and she was in Bethlehem in obedience to the empire's demand for a census. She was obedient even to her tyrannical rulers' legal and legitimate demands.

Mary's virtues began even farther back: in her love of God the Father. But if love is giving to another, what can we give to God? We cannot give God anything He needs, because He is perfect and needs nothing. But there is one thing we can give to God that He passionately wants, even though He does not need it: our free love and adoration. That is the one and only thing that He cannot give to Himself! Even omnipotence cannot do that, because a love that is forced is a contradiction in terms.

Mary's virtue begins there, with her love of God, and flows from there, since it is God who set up and authorized and commanded the whole system of virtues, rights, and duties that is human morality. This is why the Jews loved the divine law even though it showed them up as sinners, as a strong light shows up all our warts and wrinkles: because the law was God's will, and if they loved God, then they loved His will—because it was His. That is "religion", which means "relationship". It is personal, not impersonal. As Buber so perfectly put it, the moral law for them was not an "I-It" relationship but an "I-Thou" relationship. The moral law was not an imposition on life or an addition to life; it was the law of life itself. Morality and life were one thing, not two things. Only when we do abstract philosophizing about ethics do we see them as two things. Mary did not do this. Her *not*-philosophizing was not a defect but a perfection. In fact, it was the highest philosophizing.

5. Humility

Augustine, asked to name the four cardinal virtues, replied: "Humility, humility, humility, and humility." As pride is the primal sin, humility is the primal virtue. God often withholds from us the grace to overcome any and all other sins for that reason: because He sees that if we did, we would become proud of it, and then "the last state of that man becomes worse than the first" (Mt 12:45).

But can we not become proud of our humility? Yes, like the Pharisees, who, Christ said, were on their way to Hell (Mt 23:33). As Pascal said, there are only two kinds of people: the righteous, who know they are sinners, and sinners, who think they are righteous. The most dangerous of all sins is to resist the most humbling of all truths, which is our great comfort when it is accepted and our great condemnation when it is denied, namely, the truth that we do not deserve to be saved, that we are totally dependent on mercy, not justice.

I think God allowed the great tragedy of the Protestant Rebellion (the Reformation really happened at the Council of Trent) because many Catholics had forgotten this liberating biblical and Catholic truth, and it took the heretic Luther to remind them of it. Of course the Bible is very clear that although we are saved by mercy, not justice, we are not justified by faith alone (Jas 2:24), that a faith that does not produce good works, i.e., the works of love, is a fake faith. All heresies emphasize one truth against another, whether the heresies are believed by Protestants or Catholics.

Mary's humility is shown by the fact that she was "troubled" at the angel's salutation. For being praised troubles the humble and pleases the proud. And, therefore, she was troubled (a) because God's angel came to *her*; (b) because he saluted her with a formal, respectful "hail!", (c) because he called her "full of grace", (d) because he said that God Himself was "with you", and (e) because of the extraordinary and extravagant predictions about her son (Lk 1:32–33).

6. Mary's Philosophy of Law and Obedience

We use the same word ("law") for moral laws, physical laws, and mathematical laws. But physical laws are simply descriptions of how physical things do in fact behave, not laws about how persons ought to behave. And mathematical laws are not about behavior at all but about necessary and unchangeable relationships between abstract quantities. We may be able to argue from physical and/or mathematical laws to the existence of a divine Mind that designed them— that argument is quite difficult, abstract, controversial, and disputable—but the argument from an absolute moral law to an absolute moral lawgiver, from the experience of being under the law of right and wrong, like all human beings, to the existence of a more than human will behind that objective and universal and absolute moral law, is much easier and more obvious, though it, too, can be denied if you really, desperately want to get out of the uncomfortable position of being morally responsible for your sins.

The concept of right is relative to the concept of law. What is right is defined by law.

What premoderns meant by "right" was not primarily "rights" that attach to persons and that impose duties on other persons to respect those rights, but simply that which is the right thing to do. It is defined by law, so that it becomes almost a synonym for obedience. And when the law is God's perfect Law, it is a synonym for obedience.

Laws are like words. Words do not come from nowhere; they come from the minds and mouths of those who speak them. And words do not move into nothingness; they move, like arrows, into targets, which are the minds and ears of those who hear them. Laws are to the will what words are to the mind. They express the will of the lawgiver, and they are addressed to the will of the law-obeyer or disobeyer. Both laws and words are interpersonal.

Here Mary's femininity shows. Men tend to use reason to look at the law and to define right (and good and also duty) as obedience to law. And this is true, and Mary does not disagree. But men also tend to look at the law itself rather than the persons involved, and when they do look at the persons, they look at the relationship between persons and laws, not between persons and persons. Women are more "personalistic" and tend to look at laws as personal transactions, as analyzed above by the analogy to words. This difference is, of course, a difference in degree, not a difference in kind. But women tend more to look at the person behind the law. Their relationships are primarily personal, and they interpret laws (and words, too) in relationship to persons rather than interpreting and judging persons in terms of laws, as men tend to do. Thus, they are more likely than men to seek a "personal relationship with God", the giver of the moral law, and less likely to be legalists, who absolutize the law, especially the Law of God. They also tend more to mercy, especially when they look at the other relationship between persons and laws, namely, the relationship between the law and the persons *under* the law. They are more willing to make exceptions and look at mixed motives.

Mary combines both in her wonderful summary of all morality. Her last words in Scripture, addressed to the servers at Cana after she said to Jesus "They have no wine" and He apparently denied her request, were these: "Do whatever he tells you." In those five words is contained the whole of Christian morality. There is nothing else.

This precept contains both moral absolutism ("Do *whatever* he tells you") and relativism (for the "whatever" is relative to Him not He to it).

When Christ reduced the whole of the Law of Moses to the two laws of love, He was doing essentially the same thing as Mary did at Cana. Law is impersonal, while love is interpersonal, not impersonal. The impersonal is relative to the personal. Things are only means; persons are ends. The reason we are to keep the commandment against adultery, e.g., is for the sake of the persons, the spouse and the children. If my wife asked me: "Why have you been faithful to me for sixty years?" and I answered: "Because I want to obey the sixth commandment", that would be a terrible personal insult.

So the moral law of "right" is defined by love (*agape*), not love by right. To love the law and the righteousness of the law but not the person is not to be in the right at all. To be merely right, like the Pharisees, is to be wrong.

But what is love? For our modern post-Christian apostate culture, which worships feelings, love is a feeling. For Christianity, love is not a feeling but a doing. That is why it is commanded; feelings cannot be commanded. And that is why it makes promises. We cannot promise to keep feeling a certain way. We can promise to keep doing. "Actions speak louder than words"—and also louder than feelings. That is clear from Christ's parable of the two sons who were commanded by their father to work for him that day: one both felt and (therefore) said: "No, I will not", but did, while the other felt and (therefore) said: "Yes, I will" but did not. Christ asked: Which of the two did his father's will (Mt 21:28–31)?

The definition of love in words is found in 1 Corinthians 13. There, feelings are ignored. The definition of love in action is found on the Cross. There, feelings are crucified. The first is the essence of the Word of God on paper, and the second is the essence of the Word of God on wood.

Did Mary *feel* like seeing her bleeding, dying Son on the *via dolorosa* and on the Cross? Did she feel like giving Him up to a life of martyrdom when she presented Him to God in the Temple and when she let Him go to begin His public ministry by performing the Cana miracle? Did Christ "feel good about himself" in Gethsemane? Was the message He preached on the Cross "I'm O.K., you're O.K."? A trusted friend told me he had literally heard that preached in a Good Friday homily! That is beyond stupid; that is appalling.

"Appalling" is the right word. Someone once said he preferred Norman Vincent Peale's famous book *The Power of*

Positive Thinking to the stringent, negative, "judgmental" condemnations of sin in Saint Paul. Some wag wisely replied that he, on the other hand, found Paul appealing and Peale appalling.

7. The Rosary as the Laws of Love

If the essence of moral rightness is love, where can we see love in the concrete? In the lives of Jesus and Mary, the highlights of which are summarized in the Rosary.

Its unity is there, and it is very simple. It is the identity of God, love, and the supreme good, right, and duty. Here are three equations: (I) "God = the supreme good". (II) "God = love (*agape*)." (III) "Love = the supreme good." Any one of these three truths logically follows from the other two. It is like a three-part equation. That is the heart of ethics and the answer to its first and most important question: What is the greatest good? Concretely, the greatest good is God. Abstractly, the greatest good is love. And since God is love, it is possible that even those who do not know or believe in or obey God but who know and believe in and obey love (*agape*) are saved because they are in fact knowing, believing, and obeying God even though they do not know it. They have *kennen* knowledge but not *wissen* knowledge. Is that likely? God only knows. (See Lk 13:23–24.)

Mary shows, in her life, her actions, and her choices, the laws of love in the mysteries of her Rosary.

The First Joyful Mystery, the Annunciation: Her *fiat* to God's Word and will is the very essence of *agape* love. Love chooses. Love wills. Love says Yes to God's Word (in the mind) and God's will (in the will). And perfect love says Yes with its *whole* heart and soul and mind and strength (Mt

22:36–38). (That also includes feelings and desires ["heart"] and actions ["strength"], for their captain and commander is the will.)

The Second Joyful Mystery, the Visitation: Because it obeys the first and greatest commandment, the love of God, love necessarily also obeys the second, the love of neighbor, since that is God's commandment. The first commandment is put first and the second commandment is put second even though they are equally necessary, because God will always send you to your neighbor, but your neighbor will not always send you to God.

Love of "neighbor" means love of those who are nearest to you, whoever they may be, and therefore first and most especially your family, whom God has made to be your most immediate neighbors. You did not choose your family, but God did.

And this two-dimensional love, vertical and horizontal, forms a cross. It is self-sacrificial. Sacrifice is the truest and toughest test of true love. But it is also the simple secret of joy. Joy is love's love-child. It is testable in experience: when we love, we always find joy, deep down and in the end. Therefore, in her Magnificat, Mary says "My soul *rejoices*." Scripture records not a single word of Mary to Joseph, whom she must have loved more dearly than any other merely human being in the world, and only one sentence to the angel—essentially only one word, her *fiat*—but fifty-seven words of praise and joy to God, in her Magnificat.

The Third Joyful Mystery, the Nativity: Love is fruitful. Love is creative. Love procreates. Love affirms life. Because love is not blind, because love has eyes, love can read the message of the manufacturer's label on the tushie of every baby that is born: it says: "Made in Heaven".

The Fourth Joyful Mystery, the Presentation in the Temple: Love offers itself up completely to God, and therefore it offers its most precious possession. Mary here completes her *fiat*. She here (in His "presence") and now (in the "present") offers ("presents") her gift ("present") of her precious firstborn to God. It is the first Mass, the first offering-up, the first oblation, the first sacrifice, of Christ to the Father. Mary holds nothing back, as God the Father held nothing back. He gave Christ to her for all of us, and she now gives the same Christ to Him for all of us. She could have held Him back, but she did not. Her *fiat* includes even His Cross, which was also her sword (Lk 2:35). The sword that was the Cross, which God thrust into the earth like a syringe, to give His blood to us, was the same sword that pierced her soul, too. Accepting this was Mary's free choice. It was an act, a deed, an action, and a transaction. By it she cooperated with God; she became our Co-Redemptrix.

Of course the "co" here does not mean equality but total subordination and dependence. And Mary does only what we too must do: not just passively and unwillingly receive but also actively choose to co-operate, to operate-with, to work-with God's grace. God is so gracious that He demands that we, too, be co-redeemers in that sense. He respects and demands our free choice. That is the only reason there can be a Hell.

Mary's holiness—and ours—must have begun by faith (it can never grow from any other root), but it was enacted and completed by works, the works of love (it can never produce any other fruit).

The Fifth Joyful Mystery, the Finding in the Temple: Love risks losses, but love also heals losses. On the third day of her search for her lost Jesus, she found Him. It was a small preview, interiorly, of what would happen later exteriorly, when, on the third day of her real loss on Good Friday, she received Him again in eternal resurrected form. The love that gives itself away finds itself again. Love resurrects.

The Sorrowful Mysteries: We do not know the physical details of Mary's role in the five sorrowful mysteries, but we can guess, from the clue that Scripture gives us: she was there beneath His Cross, so there is no reason to think she would not have been with him as much as possible physically as well as spiritually at every step of the way. The movie *The Passion of the Christ* showed this dramatically in her active role in His trial and on the *via dolorosa*. For the whole of her life was a *via dolorosa*, a "way of sorrow" *as well as a way of joy*. The two are not opposites, in the long run. Life's two options are not either joy or sorrow, but either great sorrows and great joys or little sorrows and little joys. For when love offers itself, it multiplies both its joys and its sorrows by how much it offers.

But what does all this have to do with ethics? Absolutely everything, for ethics is most fundamentally about the greatest good, the greatest value, and that is love, and the Rosary shows the nature of love and the results of love better than any other events that have ever happened in the history of the world. Mary's love of her Lord is shown most radically in her choice to be with Him in His sufferings as much as she can. Love does not want pleasure; love wants union; love wants to share everything in the beloved's life, the sufferings as well as the joys. Mary would infinitely rather suffer with Him than have any joy without Him. Her whole joy is the with-ness. That is what love is. It is not a mysticism that denies pain, a Stoicism that ignores pain, a materialism that fears and flees pain, or a masochism that seeks pain for its own sake. It is love (*agape*), that obeys the simple law to "rejoice with those who rejoice, weep with those who weep" (Rom 12:15). (How many millions of spiritual miles away from Stoicism this is!) Mary goes with Christ to the Cross, not because it is a Cross, but because it is His.

All this applies increasingly to all five of the Sorrowful Mysteries.

The Luminous Mysteries: Scripture also tells us nothing about Mary's relation to the Five Luminous Mysteries, except for the wedding feast at Cana. But the same principles of love that we have just seen must also apply to joy, light, and glory just as much as to sorrow. Love always seeks maximal closeness. *That* is why we are to "rejoice with those who rejoice, weep with those who weep." If I do not want to share your whole life with you, I do not love you. If I say I love you but I do not want to maximize my time with you, I am a liar. What does love want? What would satisfy love? With-ness, we-ness, that unity that does not destroy the differences but fulfills them.

A feature of love that is shown at the wedding feast at Cana is that love notices. The heart directs the mind, as the physical heart pumps blood into the physical brain. That is why we usually notice things in proportion as we love them and care about them (or about their opposites, which we fear). Mary noticed that "they have no wine" even before the bridegroom, the steward, or the waiters did. And it was their job, not hers, to notice that.

Mary's last recorded words in Scripture come in this passage. Her command to the servers is also her fundamental command to us: "Do whatever he tells you." That "whatever" is the blank check that love gives. And that kind of love is also the secret of joy and peace. T. S. Eliot said that the greatest line in all of literature is Dante's: "In His will, our peace."

The Glorious Mysteries begin with the Resurrection.

What does the Resurrection show us about love? It shows us that love is stronger than death. Love seems to lose many battles, but in the end it necessarily wins the war. That is as certain as $2 + 2 = 4$. Beyond all data, beyond all history, beyond all experience, Love is eternal. The love that seems to be the most vulnerable thing in the world is in fact in the end the most invulnerable. Why? Because love—this love, *agape*—is not dependent on mortal human nature, nor is that its first cause. We receive it from God, as we receive our very being from God: the God who is love (1 Jn 4:16), as He is Being (Ex 3:14).

The Second and Fourth Glorious Mysteries: the Ascension and the Assumption: Mary's Assumption is both unique and special to her and at the same time common to her and us because, like Christ's Ascension, it shows us, in this world of visible bodies, love's invisible destiny for us, too. The Second and Fourth of the Glorious Mysteries (Christ's Ascension and Mary's Assumption) are mirror images of each other. Both make visible to our eyes in time what is true eternally: *that love is eternal*; that even now in time, when we love, we participate in eternity; and, therefore, that as the Son of God's love ascends home by its own active power, our human love, if it is a participation in His *agape*, is a participation in His eternity even now in time and when we die, will not ascend into Heaven by our own power but will be assumed ("taken up") into Heaven by that very same power, as Mary was. Mary stands for all of us here. If we live in love, we too will be assumed into Heaven, following her as she followed Him. "Following Christ" means not only living according to His will on earth but also following His very body to Heaven.

The Third Glorious Mystery: Mary's relation to the Holy Spirit, who descended upon the Church at Pentecost, is an even more intimate form of love than her relation to the Father or the Son. For she is the Father's daughter, the Son's mother, and the Spirit's spouse. These are three degrees of intimacy on a natural level that are reflected and perfected in her on a supernatural level. This is about us as well as Mary, for we, too, have received, in our collective history, by God's providential design, these three stages of love's intimacy with God. For the Father is God above us, the Son is God beside us, and the Spirit is God within us: three stages of increasing intimacy. These are also the three natural degrees of the spiritual life. We begin as children loving our parents with the love of admiration and respect for our superiors. When we become parents, we experience a deeper love for our children than our children, immature as they are, can have for us. But our relation to our spouse is even more intimate and total than our relationship to our children or our parents. As the spiritual life mirrors and perfects the natural life, Mary's life exemplifies and perfects the spiritual life.

Love always expands from privacy to community. Love does not grasp or clasp possessively but opens its hands to all, like the sun prodigally shedding its light and heat in all directions. God's sun is an image of God's Son, for both spread light and heat (truth and love) endlessly, gathering more and more children into the Holy Family, of which Mary is our mother. That is what Pentecost means.

The Fifth Glorious Mystery: The final mystery of the Rosary, Mary's coronation as Queen of Heaven, is the final triumph of Mary and of her perfect human love. Love rules Heaven. Love is the Queen of Heaven. And our essential prayer here on earth is that that kingdom of love may come on earth; that God's will may be done on earth, as it is in Heaven. For God's will is love, and nothing but love. That is what ethics, the science of the good, is most essentially and supremely about. Any ethic, such as Kant's or Stoicism's, that ignores or discounts love, however high and holy and noble it may be in other ways, has simply failed to answer life's most important question. If those philosophers had met Mary, she would have corrected them.

8. Mary's Philosophy of Duty

(More time has been spent in this book on an exposition of the dimensions of wisdom in general than on Mary's unique wisdom, since we know only a few of the details of her life. But since she was sinless, she must have been "the complete package", so everything in this book is about her. The following section is even more general and less specific about Mary, but its general principles are just as certain and important for understanding her.)

We know morality by conscience. Conscience is a knowing, first of all. It is an intuitive knowing rather than a logical proof, calculation, induction, or deduction. Like language, we learn it gradually, but from the beginning, it is innate in us, part of our essential human "nature". It radically distinguishes us from all other animals. If either conscience or language were not innate in us, part of our "specific difference" or essence, then we would observe two consequences that we never observe: some of us would not have them, and some animals would. When we see a human being without the powers of language or conscience, we use surgery or psychiatry to heal him, and it is sometimes successful. It never is with animals. (There are actually many otherwise seemingly sane scientists and philosophers today who deny this blatant empirical fact.)

Moral decision making is an application of this intuitive knowing that we call "conscience", and this application, unlike conscience itself, requires doubt, investigation, and reasoning, both inductive and deductive. That doubting presupposes that knowing, for doubting is an act of knowledge: you have to know what and why you are doubting. That investigation to discover new moral truths presupposes old moral truths, such as the moral value of opening your mind and exercising your "will to truth" and sacrificing time, convenience, and perhaps money to find it. That reasoning to prove a conclusion necessarily presupposes premises that are not proved, as every runner begins and ends at a fixed start and finish line and as every building stands on a foundation that is not built, namely, the ground.

Conscience includes at least three dimensions: first, a knowing of the essential and indefinable meaning of the very word "good"; secondly, a knowing that the practice and living of this moral goodness is an absolute moral duty, or obligation, that presses upon our moral will and will not go away—that we "ought" to do the good; and third, a knowing of what kinds of actions in general (though not in all particulars) are morally good and obligatory. (The Ten Commandments summarize this third thing.)

These three dimensions are all dimensions of moral *knowing*. Conscience is essentially a knowing. But it is also a feeling. We *know* the truth that we ought to do good, but we also *feel* the obligation, we feel "duty-bound" to do it. This is essentially the feeling of being "under" obligation, under moral, but not physical, necessity, of being absolutely "bound". A morality that is totally relativistic and subjective is not an inferior morality; it is not morality at all.

Other feelings usually accompany this essential feeling but are not always present and are changeable when they are;

and these may include, e.g., resentment or gratitude, discomfort or comfort, angry rebellion or honest attempts at obedience, desolation or consolation.

After a moral choice is made, two other feelings arise: the self-condemnation of guilt after having knowingly violated the moral law and self-approval after obeying it. This self-approval may be humble and grateful or proud and arrogant. And the guilt feelings may be accurate or inaccurate. Sometimes they are inaccurate because they are too strong, but usually they are inaccurate because they are too weak.

That is one of the reasons we need Purgatory: to see and feel the full weight and harm that all of our sins truly have. Truth, especially moral truth, is eternal and inescapable. If we are not totally morally "educated" on earth, we need Purgatory before we can be perfect in Heaven.

Our fundamental choice is between truth and untruth, light and darkness. All who seek truth will find it. Heaven is total truth. Even Hell is truth: truth known too late and in rebellion. The very same thing that blesses and blisses the blessed in Heaven is what tortures those in Hell: truth, especially the truth of love, which is the very nature of God. Purgatory is also truth: truth known the hard way but in time.

Duty, like right, is ultimately personal. If we have done our essential moral duty during our lives, we will hear from God our Father, "Well done, good and faithful servant; enter into the joy of your Lord." It is to Him that we are, in the long run, duty-bound, even in our duties to each other.

Duty is not only personal in their subjects but also interpersonal in their objects. We have duties, not to goods or virtues or laws or obligations, all of which are abstract, but to persons, who are concrete. (God is not abstract but concrete [though not material]. "Godliness" and "divinity" are abstract. That is why "God" and "humanity" are not correlative; "God" and "man" are. "Divinity" and "humanity" are correlative. To say "God and humanity" is like saying "Divinity and John Smith" or "the nature of a cat and Lassie the dog".)

Our duty to human persons is specified in the Ten Commandments. The first commandment in the second table of the Law is our duty to love, respect, and obey our parents. Saint Paul notes that this is the first commandment with a promise attached to it (Eph 6:2). If we do not learn our moral duty in our families, we will have an extraordinarily difficult time learning it anywhere else. If you do not love your family, how can you love strangers? If you do not love those who love you, how can you love those who do not?

We misunderstand this largely if we confuse love with a feeling. Even if your parents do not express loving feelings to you, even if they express negative feelings, even if they seriously harmed you, still they are your parents, and that means that they loved you enough to give you the most precious thing there is: your own real existence as a human person, with a body and a mind and a free will.

God invented the family. He did not have to. We could have been created as mature, individuated angels. The family is the institution that most incarnates self-giving love. We exist only because our parents gave that gift to us, and it is impossible to give them back anything that great, so we "pay it forward" by giving our children the gift our parents gave us. The family is "the pay-it-forward system".

And, of course, Mary is the perfect example. She is totally "into" her holy family, especially her only Son. That is why she does not assert herself. Even in Heaven she will continue to point beyond herself to Him. There is no prayer that she more delights to answer than "Show us the blessed fruit of thy womb, Jesus." Like God the Father, she gives up her only Son for us, her spiritual children. She "pays it forward", she passes on the Gift. From the Annunciation, through the Presentation in the Temple, to Christ's beginning His public ministry by His Baptism, to His first miracle at Cana, and to His sending out the seventy disciples to preach, in each step of His ministry Mary kept giving Him away. And the Church (which, as Saint John Paul II loved to say, is "Marian before she is Petrine") keeps doing the same thing in every Mass and Holy Communion.

We began this section by exploring duty and ended by exploring love. That is no accident, for our first duty is to love. Christianity makes love a duty, and this does not make love dry and impersonal. As Kierkegaard points out in *Works of Love*, this makes love eternal. When love (*agape*) and duty meet, love does not change, but duty does.

Chapter X

MARY'S POLITICAL PHILOSOPHY

This chapter will be the shortest, for two reasons. First, because there is very little evidence for anything that could be called Mary's political philosophy. Second, because that is precisely the positive point about it: that it is not as important as we think it is, or was, or should be, or should have been. Christianity, unlike Confucianism, Islam, and ancient biblical Judaism, is not wedded to a specific political system, though it does contain important principles that are political. But when we speak of Christian political principles, the politics are not essential to the principles, but the principles are essential to the politics.

When faith in God declines, faith in the state always arises to step into the vacuum. We have to worship something or someone as our absolute, and when "God is dead" in a culture, He is never replaced by the vacuum of "neutrality". Life is inescapably spiritual warfare, and Christ says that "he who is not with me is against me" (Mt 12:30) spiritually, even if this is not true militarily or politically, and even though compromise is often necessary and justified politically.

We may think that our new god is sex, but perhaps it is politics. For even sex is politicized today. What sex delivers today (in its contracepted form) is only pleasure, while politics delivers power. And if we have power, we can control everything, including pleasure. Kierkegaard wrote, in his *Journals*, that if he asked his servant for a glass of water and the servant brought him a glass of delicious wine, he would fire the servant to teach him that true pleasure is "getting my own way". Power is an aphrodisiac.

As Augustine pointed out in *The City of God*, the all-time classic of Christian politics and history, there are only two kinds of people: those whose God is God and whose love is directed to Him and those whose god is themselves and this-worldly goods (pleasure, power, honor, glory, wealth, etc.). Whenever we relativize religion, whether in ancient Rome or in modern America, we tend to absolutize politics. You might say that religion is God's politics, and politics is man's religion. Most Christians today (I write this in 2019) either hate and fear Donald Trump more than the Devil, or else, they see him as the Messiah. We are much more passionate, and certainly more public, about our political beliefs than about our religious beliefs.

And we tend to emphasize those aspects of our religion that coincide with our politics. These can be either "Left-wing" or "Right-wing", though the "Left", for reasons in its own ideology, tends to absolutize politics and the desire to expand the state's control of individual lives more than the "Right" does. A century ago the most prominent difference between Left and Right was between Nazism, i.e., National Socialism, and Communism, i.e., international socialism. Today, the "Right" usually connotes, not a totalitarianism, but an individualism, or "libertarianism", which is the polar opposite of socialism. Most forms of both Left and Right have always been seen as dangerous half-truths by traditional Catholic social philosophy and by all the papal encyclicals.

This political philosophy has no ideological label, but it may be called "personalistic communitarianism". Its main principle is that political systems, institutions, and policies are to be judged by the good of persons, not vice versa. Thus, politics is dethroned, for the whole purpose of the state is to serve persons, for states do not have immortal souls or intrinsic value, but all persons do. Thus Christianity is the eternal enemy of totalitarianism. On the other hand, individuals are obligated to work, and to sacrifice, for the common good, especially for the poor and the disenfranchised or oppressed.

The most prominent and most distinctive theme in Catholic political philosophy is the superiority of the Church (which is for eternity) over the state (which is for ever-changing times) and, therefore, the need for the Church to be free and independent from secular control. The misapplication of this principle in the past often led to the desire to unite these two powers ("Caesaro-papism"), and this typically meant the Church's lusting after the prostitute of political power. That is why nearly everyone supports "the separation of Church and state" today, though for opposite reasons: secularists fear the state's corruption by the Church, the corruption of politics by religion; while believers fear the Church's corruption by the state, the corruption of religion by politics.

Where does Mary fit in? Mary, as a Jew, was part of a "church", a "called-out people", which was a visible institution, like the Catholic Church. Israel was not just an "invisible church" of the spirit. In fact, Israel was so "political" that it had its own guardian angel, Michael (see Dan 10:13). Angels are involved in politics, and God is, too. (They are *His* angels, after all!)

And so is Mary, especially today. All the major Marian apparitions (of which there have been many) all have a very concrete political dimension. At Guadalupe, her work of converting five million Mexicans required the preliminary military work of Cortés and his conquistadores' cleansing of Aztec Devil worship and human sacrifice. (See Warren Carroll's *Our Lady of Guadalupe and the Conquest of Darkness.* See also the close parallel to the case of the Canaanites.) At Fatima, she warned specifically about Russia and Communism; at Zeitoun, the most widely witnessed miracle in history, she appeared to two million people on the dome of a Byzantine cathedral for a week, making peace signs to Muslims and Christians, whom she surely saw as future victims of Islamist terrorism.

Mary was involved in what we may call spiritual politics because Israel was not just a state (in fact it was NOT an independent state) but a "church" that was both a visible institution and an essential part of her spiritual identity. And Israel was being oppressed by a tyranny that tolerated all religions only as long as they worshipped Caesar as their god as well as their own gods. Rome therefore persecuted only Jews, and then Christians, because they were the only ones who would not embrace the idolatry of worshipping Caesar. Mary was, of course, neither a political activist nor a political theorist; but she could not help being "political", since as a Jew she was one of Rome's political victims.

The clearest example of this political involvement in her life is King Herod's holocaust of the innocents when Jesus was born and the Holy Family's flight into Egypt and exile. This act of disobedience to their political authorities implicitly appealed to the same principle as the apostles did when they were commanded by their religious authorities, the Sanhedrin, to stop preaching the Gospel. The principle was very simple: "We must obey God rather than man." In other words, Mary's last saying, "Do whatever he tells you" (at Cana), applies to politics, too. Caesar is not Lord; Christ is Lord. (That three-word formula was the first Christian creed: see 1 Cor 12:3). And this God turns man's politics upside down. This is the revolutionary point of Mary's Magnificat.

This is deeply threatening to political idolaters, for it means that since God is the Lord, therefore Caesar, Herod, the Senate (Roman or American), the Supreme Court, or the president is not.

Mary had all the virtues; therefore, she had patriotism too. Patriotism is a virtue because it is an extension of our respect for our parents and ancestors. But our loyalty to the state is subordinate to our loyalty to our family and to God. (Significantly, the same word "piety" (*pietas*) meant both of those things together in ancient Latin: respect for family and for the gods.) We are loyal to our state because of God, because God delegated His authority not only to our parents and ancestors but also to our nation. ("The [powers] that exist have been instituted by God", says Saint Paul [Rom 13:1], and this remains true even when those powers are abused. Saint Paul wrote these words under the tyrannical Roman Empire, which had ceased to be a republic a hundred years earlier.)

If you read Mary's Magnificat alertly, it will be strikingly clear that she understood the fundamental political paradox, which is that only when a state lays down its authority at God's feet does it receive real authority. And only then does it receive free, happy, and willing obedience, as distinct from servile, fearful, and reluctant obedience from its citizens. Thus, paradoxically, the more a state abuses its authority and becomes totalitarian, the less authority it really has. For "authority" is not merely power, but the power of the right, what the Chinese call *te*, or spiritual power. "Authority" means that right makes its own might; tyranny means that might claims to make its own right. Authority enforces justice; tyranny justifies force.

This political paradox is simply the social dimension of the fundamental spiritual paradox that to lose your life for God is to gain it; to grasp your life for yourself is to lose it. Ironically, if you lust after power, you will be a weakling. Bullies are always cowards, politically as well as individually. There is no double standard between individual morality and political morality at their center, only at their periphery (where, e.g., nonresistance to evil and the embracing of martyrdom, which can be heroism when an individual practices it, become irresponsibility when a *nation* does not resist aggression, for we have a right to yield our own life up if we choose, but we do not have the right to yield up the lives of others for whom we are responsible).

Chapter XI

MARY'S PHILOSOPHY
OF HISTORY

1. Who Is the Lord of History?

When we read a novel or see a play, one of the first questions we ask about it is who wrote it and what was his purpose and point. History is a drama that is very much like a large novel or play, and the first question about it is about its Author: Who is it and what is his point?

The first question about history, then, is: Whose is it? Is it His-story or is it ours? Who is in charge here? Is there a Lord of history? Is history, like nature, God's design, His plan? Is God writing straight with our crooked lines? Or did He leave history's lordship to the Caesars? Who is the lord of history?

Jews and Christians have changed history more than anyone else because they knew that Caesar is not the lord. The earliest Christian creed was a political revolution because it implied that if "Jesus is Lord" (1 Cor 12:3), then Caesar is not.

Jews and Christians also knew that history is providential, just as much as individual lives are. That is why Saint Augustine wrote two great classics, not just one. *The City of God* is about God's Providence in history, as the *Confessions* is about God's Providence in an individual life.

245

The City of God for Mary was Israel, and then Christ's Church, which is the new Israel and does not destroy it but fulfills it (Mt 5:17). And all Israel comes to a point in Mary, like the point of an arrow, and its target is Christ. Just as all Israel's point and purpose is fulfilled in Mary, just as Mary is Israel, so Mary is the Church. Both are "she". Both are God's Bride. Both are the womb of Christ. Both give Christ to the world.

~

Nature is only the setting for the drama of life. We are its characters. God is its author. History is its plot. The plot is very long and complex, and unfinished. Is there a point, a theme, to it?

Yes, there is, and Mary's place is central. As Christ is the Second Adam, she is the Second Eve. She changes all of history! She brings God into the world! No human being ever did anything nearly as great as that. Nothing even approaches it. And this is done, not by a great Caesar or a great thinker, but by a teenage girl who calls herself "the handmaid of the Lord".

That centrality is why she figures prominently in the Book of Revelation, the symbolic basis for Augustine's *City of God* and for all subsequent Christian philosophies of history. Revelation 12 tells the story symbolically that Matthew 2:1–15 tells literally, of the slaughter of the innocents and the escape of the Holy Family into Egypt. It is central to the story's plot because it is central to the story's main character, who is its Author incarnate in the story.

2. What Is History's Plot Line?

The first question a child asks about a story is: What is it about? Is it a love story, a war story, an adventure story, a psychological drama, or what? The question presupposes that there is an answer to it and that the author of the story knows the answer, that he is in charge, that he knows what kind of story he is telling. Thus, it presupposes an answer to question 1 above, about the author.

In one sense, the story of human history is a love story. But in a fallen world, a love story is always also a war story. In fact, the single fundamental theme of every story since the Fall has always been the war between good and evil. That is the theme of the Bible, especially of its last book, Revelation, which symbolically summarizes and interprets all the little stories in terms of the big story. It is the theme of Augustine's definitive philosophy of history, which is based on the Book of Revelation.

God Himself announces this theme, within the story itself. For this God, unlike the God of deism, reveals Himself to us. In fact, He makes Himself a character in the story as well as being the transcendent Author of it. (Thus, all of God's interventions in the Old Testament, all the miracles and prophets that reveal Him, prefigure the Incarnation.)

Immediately after the Fall, which is the beginning of human history, He announces the theme of His story, of history. It is war: "I will put enmity [war] between you [Satan] and the Woman [Eve], between your seed [Herod, Pilate, Caiaphas, Rome] and her seed [Christ, the seed of Mary]; he shall bruise your head, and you shall bruise his heel" (Gen 3:15). Both bruisings were done in the same time by the same deed, the crucifixion.

This is the first Gospel, the "proto-evangelium". Strange as it sounds, the Gospel is a war story. No one can read the four Gospels alertly and intelligently and open-mindedly without seeing that. The "liberal" idea that Jesus' point and purpose was simply to teach love is about as accurate as the idea that the purpose of Adolf Hitler was to create world peace. For in a fallen world, the only way there can be love is for there to be war. Love wars. Love fights. Ask any mother, in any species of mammal, especially homo sapiens.

Christ versus Antichrist, the City of God versus the City of This World, the Holy Spirit and His angels versus the Devil and his fallen angels, light versus darkness, good versus evil—that is the plot.

And Mary is at the very center of it. As Eve was the first to fall, and was the instrumental cause of Adam's fall, so Mary is the first to be redeemed, and is the instrumental cause, through her *fiat* and her Nativity, of Christ's redemption. God said to Satan that the war would be, not merely between the first Adam and the Second Adam, but between the first Eve and her seed, beginning with Cain, and the Second Eve and her seed, beginning with Abel and culminating with Christ.

The warfare, of course, is spiritual in its root and in its essence. "We are not contending against flesh and blood, but against the principalities, against the powers, against the world rulers of this present darkness" (Eph 6:12). But because humanity is not mere spirit, mere matter, or two separate realms, as in Gnosticism, Neoplatonism, and Cartesian dualism, therefore the spiritual war is necessarily also a physical war. Thus, physical death is the inevitable consequence of spiritual death, or sin. Thus, love is not a mere intention or feeling but a lifetime of deeds. As Kierkegaard said, for a Christian love is "the works of love".

Ironically, Kierkegaard was a Lutheran. This is ironic because it was Luther who taught the doctrine of justification by faith alone (*sola fide*), not works, which is the explicit, word-for-word contradiction of Scripture (Jas 2:24)—the Scripture that Luther also taught was "alone" or sufficient in itself (*sola scriptura*). Luther denied Scripture's repeated assertions that good works (which are the works of love) are as necessary for salvation as faith.

Please do not become a Christian unless you are willing to become a warrior. To be Christ's is to be Christ's spiritual warrior. Baptism is enlistment. Unbelief is either treason or draft dodging.

And once you are enlisted and enrolled, you will be surprised to see a gentle woman as your warrior hero and the Devil's most feared enemy. Joan of Arc knew who this woman was. So did every other saint.

3. History's Greatest Protagonist at History's Greatest Crisis

If your skeptical mind is asking where in Scripture does Mary give us a philosophy of history, my answer is that Mary has much more than a book about the philosophy of history in her hand; she has history itself in her hand. She performed the single greatest, most important, most momentous deed any merely human being has ever performed in all of history. She brought God to earth. That changed *everything*. "Behold, I make *all things* new", He said (Rev 21:5)—and He never lied.

This greatest of all events, the single most amazing and important thing that has ever happened, happened in Mary, in her body, in her womb, because she said "yes". God did not do the work of redemption unilaterally or without her cooperation. God willed that her word and will were necessary to bring about the incarnation of God and the salvation of the world.

Other crucial figures in history have made some very important things new, for good or evil, but none can surpass Mary's power, for she alone, in being the indispensable instrumental cause of the Incarnation, could truly say, together with Christ, "Behold, I make *all* things new" (Rev 21:5).

4. Mary's Revolutionary Philosophy of History

Because history is His story (point #1), because only He is its lord, and not any Caesar, any warlord, or any other military, political, philosophical, scientific, or even religious revolutionary, therefore no mere man or woman who ever lived has ever performed a more revolutionary work than Mary. No one has ever changed human history more than she. No one has ever more crucially changed the life of every person who has ever lived, both in this world and in the next, than Mary.

We know more about her philosophy of history directly than about her philosophy of anything else, because we have the most words about it, in the Magnificat. Here is her philosophy of history in two parts: the part about her and the part about the world. The second is directly about the philosophy of history, but the first part is, too, indirectly, because it is about her, who is the instrumental cause of that great change in history. In both parts, she makes revolutionary claims. Like Jesus, Mary says something that, if it were not true, would make her insufferably and insanely proud and arrogant about herself: that "henceforth all generations will call me blessed." She is blessed precisely because she is humble. And the rest of the world is blessed by it, too: first, by her humility, and second, by that of all her imitators. All humble Marys will be raised up, and all the proud will be cast down, throughout history.

My soul magnifies the Lord,
and my spirit rejoices in God my Savior,
for he has regarded the low estate of his handmaiden.
For behold, henceforth all generations will call me blessed;
for he who is mighty has done great things for me,
and holy is his name.
And his mercy is on those who fear him
from generation to generation.
He has shown strength with his arm,
he has scattered the proud in the imagination of their hearts,
he has put down the mighty from their thrones,
and exalted those of low degree;
he has filled the hungry with good things,
and the rich he has sent empty away.
He has helped his servant Israel,
in remembrance of his mercy,
as he spoke to our fathers,
to Abraham and to his posterity for ever.

Notice that the subject of every single affirmation after the first one is "he". And even the first affirmation is about God, not about her. This focus would be expressed best if it were translated "The Lord is the one in whom my spirit rejoices." Put God first and yourself last, let God be God, and let yourself be His humble handmaid, and you will be so exalted that all generations will call you blessed.

This is not just an ethic but also a philosophy of history. It applies to nations as well as to individuals. Tyrants and conquerors fail; servants succeed. Givers are rewarded, takers are punished. Generous nations are blessed, like generous individuals, and selfish ones are cursed, like selfish individuals. The law is as certain for nations as for individuals.

This will apply to the history of the Church as well. The Church lives most strongly when she is willing to die. "The blood of martyrs is the seed of the Church" (Tertullian), and whenever she is a Church of martyrs, in any and all times and places, she always thrives. But when she becomes fat and rich and comfortable and stuffed with worldly power, she is corrupted and broken. Where today is the Church strongest? Where she is poorest (Africa) and most persecuted (China and Islamic countries). Where is she the weakest? Where is she dying? In "Christendom", i.e., Europe, where she was established with political power and wealth and where today ten times as many people leave her every year as enter her.

God is a revolutionary. God raises up and casts down. History, then, like individual life, is not stable, safe, or secure. It is dangerous; it is an adventure. Everything else in the universe must remain within its essential borders; everything else rests stably in its essence. Man, however, both individually and collectively, does not, because he is called by God to transcend himself; and because he has free choice, he must either lose his humanity in Hell or transcend it in Heaven. Either the Devil will suck his human life from him, like Dracula, or else Christ will give him a blood transfusion and share His divinity with him. And those two futures begin now. Indeed, that is the plot line of every life, according to Augustine.

Nothing is more dramatic than that. It is the source of all drama. It calls for what Kierkegaard calls "infinite passion", the thing most notably lacking in our post-Christian world.

Dogs do not write dramas, and they would not do so even if they had the intelligence, for no dog can lose his dogginess and sink to becoming a plant, nor can any dog rise to human life. But man can lose his humanity and his freedom, in Hell, or transcend it and participate in divinity (*theosis*), in Heaven. And we see the direction of the arc of both lives here, like falling and rising hyperbolas on the graph paper of time.

Mary's philosophy of history is revolutionary, not just because it is about God bringing about revolutions and not just because it channels history's supreme power and causality, but, even more revolutionary than that, because it revolutionizes revolution itself! It changes the very meaning of power. Power itself is turned upside down, so that force becomes weakness and defeat, while yielding, suffering, and sacrificing love becomes the true power. Humility defeats pride, and the inheritors of the earth are the meek. This is the "good news" at the heart of Jesus' message, repeated many times, especially in the Beatitudes.

Yet though Mary's philosophy is revolutionary, it is also traditional, remembering and revering ancestors, especially Abraham, the first Jew, and his "posterity". "Covenants" are inherently conservative, i.e., faithful, i.e., intergenerational ("from generation to generation"). They conquer time in time; they are not just, like contracts, for a time, but "for ever".

Covenants are promises, and promises are the single most important human activity that binds and stabilizes any community by binding together past, present, and future. "I promise you" means "You can be sure that what I do to you tomorrow will be the same as what I do to you today." Without trust in promises, nothing else holds individuals together in community.

So Mary's philosophy of history is both revolutionary and traditional, radical and conservative.

5. The Relevance of Mary's Philosophy of History for Today: The Marian Apparitions

Like Christ, Mary is alive and active in the world today. She was the bearer of divine Wisdom to the world in her body in Bethlehem two thousand years ago, but she is also the bearer of divine Wisdom to the world today in her spiritual presence to God in Heaven as our most powerful intercessor. And she continues to be God's instrument to bring Christ to the world in countless ways. She is still acting and miraculously appearing and speaking to the world. She did not retire. She does not know the meaning of retirement.

In fact, her miraculous appearances are dramatically increasing as modernity rushes faster toward the edge of its cliff.

Her solution is scandalously simple. She goes to the root of our problem, which is our ignoring of what Christ called "the great and first commandment" (Mt 22:36–38). That is what the great prophet Alexandr Solzhenitsyn also said in his 1978 Harvard Commencement address: that "men have forgotten God." (Of course he scandalized Harvard by saying that, just as Mother Teresa did a few years later.) We have relativized the absolute and absolutized the relative. In abolishing God, we have also abolished man as His image. We have reduced God to a projection of man and reduced man to an accident of evolution. In confusing ourselves with gods, we have confused ourselves with the beasts. We see ourselves both as gods, as sovereign, independent, and autonomous, and also as mere accidents of blind chance, dust of the earth in the winds of time.

This is what the two most brilliant popes of the twentieth century have said: that the crisis in our culture is about anthropology, about the image of God. If, as Nietzsche said, "God is dead", then so is His image in man. When you stand before a mirror, your image remains, but when you leave the room, it also leaves. We are living now in the split second between the abolition of God and what C. S. Lewis (another prophet) called *The Abolition of Man*.

That image of God is, among other things, sexuality, according to Genesis 3:15. That is why the Sexual Revolution is an implicit atheism: it substitutes human authority for divine authority, human invention for divine design, human ideology for divine revelation. Not only is it no longer the icon of Trinitarian love; it is no longer even "the reproductive system", it is "the entertainment system". The Pill has relabeled pregnancy as a disease and babies as "accidents".

All Marian apparitions give the same old scandalously simple solution to this complex modern problem: repent, convert, turn back to God. Pray. Say the Rosary. Her solution is the very last one a proud and autonomous culture can accept: to our culture it is childish, not "adult" (like our "adult" movies and "adult" magazines). It is "simplistic".

Our culture is scandalized by God's simplicity and enthralled by matter's complexity. For matter is maximally pluralized, spread out, complexified. "It is a complex issue" is the lie we tell ourselves about atheism, about abortion, about marriage, about virtue, about sanctity, about the meaning of life: about the only things that are in fact simple! Like our computers, we are very good at making complex things simple and easy, but we also make simple things complex.

We multiply the leaves of our diseased tree, but Mary strikes at the root. In her anthropology, as in every part of her philosophy, she addresses the practical, lived problem rather than the academic, scholarly, theoretical issues. Contrary to the popular fallacy, practice is simpler than theory. Abstract theories can be endlessly complexified, but concrete practice always comes down to a choice between good and evil. God's solution to the problem of death was simple: resurrection. God's solution to the problem of sin was simple: repentance. God's solution to the problem of damnation was simple: trust Me, love Me. To us who endlessly talk, He replies, "Shut up and dance with me."

That is what Mary did. That is also why she did not talk much. She was too busy dancing. Her Magnificat is a dance of words. All its words are festoonings of her one word to God, her *fiat*, her "be", her "yes".

6. *Mary and Communism*

To appreciate Mary's role today, we have to have a little look at contemporary history. We have won the "Cold War" against the USSR, but we have lost the real war to Communism. For the heart of Communism is not in economics. Even Communist China has compromised its Marxism in economics and compromised with capitalism, for the undeniable reason that it simply works better. But they will not compromise their atheism and their opposition to the Church. That was very clear when Xi publicly said: "We will not allow the Catholic Church in China to be independent of the control of the Communist Party." And the Pope apparently had his hearing aid turned off that day, and he bowed to Xi's demand to have the authority to choose and/or approve or refuse bishops for the Catholic Church in China in order to spare the faithful Chinese Catholics persecution. Imagine Jesus doing what His vicar did. Imagine Jesus letting Caesar appoint apostles for His Church in order to prevent the persecutions and the martyrdoms! The Chinese Communists have proved, by their actions as well as their words, that they would much rather compromise with capitalism than with Catholicism. Their choices show what their real ultimate values are. The conflict is not economic, it is religious. Even Communists understand that God is more important than money or private property, even if He does not exist!

The agreement has not, as of this writing, been allowed to be seen by the public. In other words, the Vatican is acting exactly as totalitarian tyrants act. Perhaps God will use this naïveté on the part of the pope and Machiavellian secrecy on the part of the Vatican diplomats who advise him to bring about exactly the opposite of what it was intended to bring about, namely, a greater persecution than before. That seems to be happening. And its result could well be the same in China as it was in Rome two thousand years ago. For "the blood of martyrs is the seed of the Church." God is a better strategist than His diplomats. He plays chess with them, and His gambit may be to sacrifice some weak pawns for an eventual checkmate.

The point is that the West has won the economic war— our enemy is becoming more and more like us economically—but Communism has won the spiritual war—we are becoming more like them spiritually. Throughout Western civilization, atheism and materialism are growing, and all religions except Islam are shrinking.

The Devil is a clever military strategist: he goes for our

weakest point. And it is a crucial one because it is the origin of life itself: sex. That is the major battlefield where the West is losing its soul.

The Sexual Revolution (it already has its own capital letters, like the "Pill") is more important than any economic revolution, even Communism, because we all recognize that sex is more important than money if we only analyze what is the essential mechanism of the universally popular institution of prostitution. A john gives up what he wants less, namely money, for what he wants more, namely sex. True, the prostitute gives up sex for money, but she is not made happy by that; no woman deliberately sets out to be a prostitute. But the john freely chooses to be a john because the sex makes him happy on a short-range and material level. This proves that sex is more important than money to mankind in the same way as expensive surgery proves that health is more important than money.

Communist egalitarianism is adamantly opposed to all hierarchy, both economic (capitalism) and metaphysical (supernaturalism) and also sexual. Sex is intrinsically hierarchical and not egalitarian, for women are obviously superior to men at being women, and men are obviously superior to women at being men, which allows mutual subordination and humility and respect. But Communism repudiates all hierarchy and embraces total equality, including equality of masculinity and femininity, that is, the abolition of manhood and womanhood as mere man-made cultural constructs. This is exactly the philosophy that dominates our academic culture today.

Communism is also in theory suspicious of the family, for Communism cannot tolerate any other entities, any mediating institutions, between the state and the individual, whether religion or family. Therefore, Communism is suspicious of both fatherhood and motherhood, and most adamantly the fatherhood of God and the motherhood of Mary. This is philosophically consistent with materialism, for materialism reduces everything down to matter, and in the realm of matter, there are no qualities or qualitative differences, only quantitative ones. Qualities such as fluidity in water are explained by the quantity of atoms, two hydrogen atoms rather than one. All qualities are reduced to quantities, as in the binary logic of a computer.

This demand for equality is fanatical when it comes to sex. This is happening even in America. For instance, the previously very popular Larry Summers was fired as president of the world's most prestigious educational institution (Harvard University) for the cardinal sin of suggesting, in a faculty meeting to discuss why Harvard could not attract more women to the STEM courses, an intolerable heresy: that we should be allowed to discuss whether there might possibly be any innate differences between men and women. He was sacked, not for suggesting that there really might be such a thing, but for suggesting that the question should be discussed freely. So much for freedom of thought in our culture. No public figure can avoid being sacked if he dares to suggest that the meaning of marriage has something to do with the relations between a man and a woman. If you do not believe that, just ask Israel Folau, Australia's rugby superstar who was banned from the sport for quoting Saint Paul. Or ask Google's president, who was fired for confessing that he personally believed the same heresy. Or the Evangelical couple in England whose foster children were forcibly taken away from them by the government because they confessed that they believed everything in the Bible, including its labelling of sodomy as a sin. We are increasingly living in George Orwell's *1984*, where there is a new category of crimes, namely, "thoughtcrimes". The real tyranny is the demand to control your mind, not just your body. Communism is an example of that tyranny.

Mary is the greatest enemy of Communism because she is different, unique: uniquely feminine, uniquely immaculate, uniquely supernatural, uniquely humble, and uniquely saintly. The essence of sanctity is love, of course, but as Fulton Sheen pointed out equality is the death of love. Love always bends the knee. Equals do not have love, only friendship and justice. Both the French and the Bolshevik Revolutions demanded that all people call each other by the same name, "comrades".

Mary is the antidote to the Sexual Revolution. She is a virgin and a mother; the Sexual Revolution is anti-virgin and anti-mother. It is the demand to have sex without motherhood. The foundation and lynchpin of the Sexual Revolution is contraception, which is the demand to have sex without having babies, i.e., non-virginity and non-motherhood. Abortion, our legalized Holocaust that has already murdered more innocents than all the wars in human history, is essentially backup contraception. Connect the dots.

7. Mary and Islam

In our naïve minds, Islam has replaced Communism as our number one enemy, our number one fear.

With apparently good reason. For Islam is far more formidable.

For one thing, it has more truth. It is not atheism. In fact, it is theism, and its God is the true God. The official *Catechism of the Catholic Church* says that: that Christians and Muslims worship the same God, the one true God. Of course. We both learned who God is from the same source: the Jews. All ninety-nine of the names of Allah in the Koran are also in the Bible. But Jesus' favorite name for God is not there: "Father".

Islam has piety and wisdom. "Islam" means "total surrender to God", and the peace that comes from that surrender. (The Arabic word *islam* is cognate to the Hebrew word *shalom*.) That is the heart of all true religion. Muslims in the West are usually more pious, and almost always more unbudgeable, more adamant, more passionate, and more definitive about their religion than Christians.

Islam is a Christian heresy—essentially Nestorianism, the refusal to unite the divine and the human natures in Christ. Its history is central to Christian history for 1400 years, and always polemical. Three times Islam almost conquered Christian Europe: at Tours, or Poitiers, at Vienna, and at Lepanto. All three times we were outnumbered by men but not by angels or miracles.

Islam, unlike all other religions, is committed to conquering the world. Only Muslims and Christians send out missionaries, because their two founders commanded their disciples not to rest until all were converted (Mt 28:19–20).

Another unbridgeable difference is that Christianity is not wedded to politics or to any particular political system, but Islam is. Failure in this world is, for Muslims, failure absolutely. That is why the Koran says Jesus could not have been crucified, because Allah would never allow one of his prophets to fail and to be publicly disgraced. Islam is just as adamant about conquering the world politically and militarily as National Socialism (Nazism) and international socialism (Communism) were. But it has lasted far longer than either. In fact, Islam is the only heresy that has lasted and increased and prospered for 1400 years.

In the West, Islam is rising and Christianity is falling. Both processes are accelerating. After 1400 years of failure to conquer Christendom (Europe) on the battlefield, it is now succeeding, not with swords, but with mothers. Muslims in the West are having children; Christians are not. Muslims see life as something worth living; Christians increasingly do not. For those who see life as a precious gift have children. Muslims are obeying God's first commandment to be fruitful; Christians are not. Muslims are the only people in the world, except for Orthodox Jews, Mormons, and Evangelicals, who are not massively succumbing to the Sexual Revolution. Catholics are. The rate of contraception, abortion, fornication, adultery, divorce, sodomy, and transgenderism is just as high among Catholics as among non-Catholics. Not so for Muslims.

Islam has almost completely destroyed Christianity in the Middle East, which used to house more Christians than any other part of the world. It did the same in North Africa. It is trying to do the same in sub-Saharan Africa today. That is the battleground where Muslims are the most terroristic and violent and where Christians are the most massacred and martyred—and also the most pious and the most joyful and the most growing.

But the fact that Islam is for the first time in 1400 years conquering Christendom today throughout Western Europe is only half the truth. The other half is that for the first time in 1400 years, there are many Muslim conversions to Christianity. And almost all of them involve supernatural visions of Mary. Every missionary who has worked undercover in Muslim countries for the last generation will tell you that.

Muslims love Mary. She is the ideal Muslim, the ideal "surrenderer" to God. She has "infiltrated" the religion of

Islam deeply. The Koran is very clear about her virginity and the miraculous birth of Christ. The Annunciation, the Visitation, and the Nativity are in the Koran. In chapter 19, there are forty-one verses about Mary and her Son. She is "the most blessed of all women". Muhammad's own daughter Fatima is only second. Fatima says: "I surpass all the women except Mary." Our Lady of Fatima ranks higher than Fatima. It is an obvious trick of Divine Providence to have Mary's most striking, famous, and important supernatural appearance to the modern world take place in a town named for Muhammad's daughter.

At Fatima, Portugal, seventy thousand people, including many atheists and skeptics, saw the miracle of the sun. The town of Fatima was named after the daughter of the last Muslim chief in Portugal (who in turn was named after Muhammad's daughter) after centuries of Muslim occupation, toward the end of the seven-hundred-year long war to liberate Iberia from Muslim control. A Catholic boy loved this Muslim woman Fatima and persuaded her to marry him and remain in Portugal when all the other Muslims retreated. She became a Catholic, and her husband loved her so much that he named his hometown after her.

There are no coincidences.

About eighty years later, Mary's week-long appearance on the dome of a cathedral in Zeitoun, a suburb of Cairo, was witnessed by over two million people, mostly Muslims, but also Coptics, Orthodox, and Catholics. Far more people witnessed this miracle than any other miracle in history. Mary said no words but made signs of peace to both Muslims and Christians. Mary is the Queen of Peace because her Son is the Prince of Peace. What do you think she feels about the fact that the two religions that love her the most are so often at war with each other? What does a loving mother feel when she sees her children hating and fearing each other?

Both Islam and the West, having forsaken the divine Christ for different reasons, may still revere the human Mary. Islam, having from its beginning rejected Christ's divinity, has nevertheless always revered Mary. She is our loving spy, and her Son will listen to her prayers as he did at Cana. If he can turn water into wine, he can turn terrorists into saints, haters into lovers, heretics into the faithful. For Mary knows how to fight better than Muslims do. She knows that the weapons of love are stronger than those of hate, even if her children do not. Today Muslims believe in strength but not love, and Christians believe in love but not strength. They are like the Cross without Christ, for they are willing to die for their faith. We are like Christ without the Cross because we are not. What happens to those who put the two together? Like the martyrs, they will conquer the world.

How? Not as Alexander the Great did, and as Muslims have consistently tried to do, by arms. Not as Buddha did, by denying its existence or its importance. But as Christ did, by giving themselves up for it. Mary is the first in this line; whoever follows her most closely will be the first to conquer the world.

Chapter XII

MARY'S PHILOSOPHY
OF ART AND BEAUTY

Spiritual beauty is greater than physical beauty, just as spiritual joys and sorrows are greater than physical joys and sorrows. And therefore the most beautiful thing in the universe is a saint. Mary, the only immaculate one, is therefore the most beautiful thing in the universe. To quote the beautiful Akathist Hymn of the Orthodox, Mary is "more honorable than the cherubim, and beyond compare more glorious than the seraphim." Mary is God's greatest work of art, God's masterpiece. She is the archetype, touchstone, and standard of all beauty. She is the concretization of what Scripture calls "the beauty of holiness" (1 Chron 16:29; Ps 29:2, 96:9 KJV).

Beauty is the child of truth and goodness, honesty and love, and beauty's child is joy. The greatest joy we get from beauty comes, not from physical causes, but from spiritual causes, though even the physical beauties and joys are so great and powerful that they sweep our spirits away like a tsunami. Our greatest joy comes from our greatest beauties, which are spiritual: our love of truth and goodness.

The most beautiful thing in life is love. Therefore, love is also the most joyful thing in life, for beauty is the cause of joy. And the most beautiful form of love is self-forgetful. That is ecstasy in both senses of that word: (1) "standing-outside-yourself", and (2) supreme joy. Christ incarnates this love most perfectly, and no one was closer to Christ than Mary.

God is the First Cause of all beauty as well as the First Cause of all truth (through the *Logos*, the Mind of God) and the First Cause of all goodness, i.e., love, (through the Holy Spirit, who is the love between the Father and the Son and who is the sanctifier, the saint-maker).

Art is the creation and expression of beauty. God's art masterpiece is Mary, and Mary, in turn, is the greatest human artist, both with her life (since sanctity is the greatest art and contains the greatest beauty) and with her words.

What words? Lovers know that the two most eloquent languages of love are silence and music.

Mary, like Christ, has very few words, and most of them, in her Magnificat, are poetry, which is word-music. For she is most Christlike, and no one ever condensed more beauty, truth, goodness, and meaning into fewer words than Christ: e.g., the Beatitudes, the Lord's Prayer, and the Seven Words from the Cross. Mary's comparative silence is like His because her love is like His.

And Mary's music is like His music, also. What is His music? He is the *logos*, the "word" or expression of the Creator, and the human art that comes closest to that expressive art is music. That was the language that God spoke to create the world. Even today, we rightly call music "the universal language". It is probably the language we will all speak and understand in Heaven, when the babble of Babel is undone. Even here on earth, we all sense that there is hidden meaning in music that simply cannot be put into words. It cannot be reduced to, relativized to, or translated into any other medium. Music makes us mystics. It is more Godlike than any other art. That is why it touches our hearts more deeply than any other art.

Mary is like music.

How? In the same way that she is like the moon. It is often (and rightly) said that Mary is like the moon in that all her light is reflected from the sun, the Son of God. It is even more rightly said that Mary is like music, and music is like Mary. For if God were dead, as Nietzsche said, then music would go deaf and dumb because it would have no one to praise. Thus, the existence of music proves the existence of God.

Mary's Magnificat, like her life, is all praise. Praise is the highest function of music.

The fullest music is song, for the human voice is the most beautiful musical instrument. And the most beautiful songs are songs of praise to God the Father, inspired by the Spirit and coming from the heart, and working through the medium of the *Logos*, the Son, the Mind of God.

Mary *sings* her words. All her words, not only her Magnificat. *Fiat* is a song-word. It is the same word ("Be!") that God sang to bring creation into being. Mary reflected it and, thus, brought redemption into being.

The greatest of our music is a series of echoes of the music of Eden. (Does truly great music not often seem like that to you?) Mary's namesake, Miriam, Moses' sister, also sang, after the Red Sea crossing. And Deborah sang after she defeated Sisera and the Canaanites (Judges 4 and 5). And Simeon the prophet sang the "Nunc Dimittis" at the Presentation (Lk 2:22–32).

Songs are free. In Psalm 137, the captive slaves in Babylon could not sing the songs of Jerusalem in the land of slavery. They hung their harps on Babylon's trees because they hung their hearts in Jerusalem's Temple.

Mary sings for joy (Lk 1:47). Joy is not just happiness. Happiness is peace and contentment, but joy is more than peace and contentment. Happiness is a smile; joy is a song.

Will Heaven be full of music or full of silence? Both, at

the same time. The question is wrong. It is like the question: Will Heaven be serious or funny? The answer to that question is: You can't be serious!

If you do not understand that, see Pasolini's flawed but fascinating film *The Gospel According to St. Matthew* just for the scene where Joseph comes back to Mary after the angel tells him where her baby came from. The smile on her face when she sees him coming is even better than the one on the Mona Lisa. It is to joy what the *Pietà* is to sorrow. It will break your heart. That is the purpose of beauty: to break your heart.

Chapter XIII

MARY'S PHILOSOPHY
OF EDUCATION

Education is crucial to human life, and, therefore, one's philosophy of education is a very important part of one's philosophy. Plato famously said, in the *Republic*, that good education is the one thing that is most necessary for a good society. For even if all the relations between persons and institutions were good at the present, if they are not passed down to the future by education, they are ephemeral and would be lost forever. Military invasions conquer space, but education conquers time.

The first question in education is the "what" question. What do we teach? And the Christian answer, like the Jewish answer, is, of course, tradition, "the deposit of faith", or the wisdom that has come from God through our ancestors and through God's direct dealings with His people, especially as recorded in their Sacred Scriptures. Like Jews everywhere, Mary was a traditionalist. That is the secret of progress, as the foundation is the secret of a stable building.

The next question is method, which we have already explored in chapter 1, where we found the rabbinic (and Socratic) method of questioning both in Mary's practice (questioning the angel: Lk 1:34) and in Christ's (in the Temple at twelve: Lk 2:46). Active "pondering" was also a part of her method. It was a kind of interior dialogue, a mirror of the rabbinic questioning and answering.

But the most important question in education is not what or how but who. Every student remembers not so much the lesson as the teacher.

Wisdom Himself sat on Mary's lap as His throne. She had the world's best teacher. But she first had to teach Him. She had to teach the Eternal Word of God to speak Hebrew, to imitate her obediently! For Scripture says that He was "obedient" to Mary and Joseph (Lk 2:51). We learn, first of all, through obedience. And since Christ was like us in all things but sin (cf. Heb 4:15), therefore He, too, had to learn obedience, first through Mary and Joseph, then through suffering (Heb 5:8).

God Incarnate learned to obey His human mother and his human foster father. What humility! What power Mary had! Only innocence could possibly possess it without being corrupted. And after she was His teacher, she was His student. Surely He taught her many, many things, some of them in words. Of this hidden life, Cardinal Newman says: "Mary for thirty continuous years saw and heard Him, being all through that time face to face with Him, and being able to ask Him any question which she wished explained, and knowing that the answers she received were from the Eternal God, who neither deceives nor can be deceived." And this seeing and hearing Him was active on her part, as Newman explains: "She does not think it enough to accept, she dwells upon it ['ponders'] . . . it is not enough to assent, she develops it; not enough to submit the reason, she reasons upon it."

Who were Mary's students? The whole family of mankind. She has been appearing so repeatedly in modern times because we are very severely retarded and rebellious students who desperately need her education. She is the primary "special needs teacher".

She, and not just her dead example, is actively doing this. She is not dead, any more than Christ is. She is much more alive now in Heaven than she ever was on earth, and she is acting and intervening in the world through her intimate intercession with Christ. Her means and methods are not power and fear and force but truth and love, in other words, education.

But education is like dancing: "it takes two to tango." The teacher is doing her part, but the students are not listening.

Chapter XIV

MARY'S PHILOSOPHY
OF RELIGION

Even philosophers, however secular they are (and they are usually very secular today), recognize that religion is an important dimension of many human lives, so they philosophize about it, as they do about politics, education, history, art, etc. But it is usually treated as a foreign, arcane, and antique cultural artefact, from the standpoint of a visitor to a zoo studying the animals. Mary would be as incomprehensible to them as they would be to her.

Obviously, Mary does not have a theoretical, academic philosophy of religion that addresses the usual questions, such as attempts to prove or disprove the existence of God and the immortality of the soul by syllogistic arguments. But she has definite, life-changing answers to the practical, concrete questions of religion, especially the most central and essential one, namely, how can we have a lived religion, i.e., relationship (for that is what the word literally means) with God?

The Essential Issue

She not only teaches us the answer to this question, she becomes the answer. For she not only reveals but also actually brings about the essence of our religion, the union of God with us ("Emmanuel"), first by her *fiat*, which allows the

Incarnation, bringing Him down from Heaven to earth, and then by her Nativity, bringing Him out of her womb and into our world. And still today, she brings us to God and God to us by her most powerful intercession with her divine Son. None of the millions of other teachers in the world can do the first two things, and although all of them can do the third thing, none can do it as powerfully as she can.

"Religion" is essentially "relationship", and Mary exemplifies perfectly, in her own person, the three most intimate of all human relationships toward the three Persons of the Trinity: she is the perfect daughter of the Father, the perfect mother of the Son, and the perfect spouse of the Holy Spirit.

Her motherhood to the Son is unique, but in the other two of these Trinitarian relationships, she shows the way for us, too, for we, too, are God's children, and we, too, are invited into the spiritual marriage whose result is *theosis*, a two-becoming-one, a participation in the very divine nature and divine life, a spiritual marriage of the human and the divine in the single human person that we are, so that we become "little Christs".

Very, *very* little Christs, indeed, but nevertheless little *Christs*, not just little Caesars or little Socrateses. In Christ, this marriage of the divine and the human is complete, perfect, eternal, and by nature, while ours is incomplete, imperfect, ever growing, and by grace. But it is the same thing, as a two-year-old taking her first clumsy dance step and the most perfect ballerina in the world are doing the same thing.

The twelve most important events in Mary's life are all "religious", or God-relational, through her uniquely intimate and complete association with the God-made-man. There are twelve close parallels or analogies between Christ and her:

(1) Her Immaculate Conception in time paralleled His immaculate and eternal begottenness from His Father.

(2) Her *fiat*, or "yes", or "amen" to God's angel at the Annunciation parallels and echoes Christ's "yes" to the Father both in eternity and in time. He came into the world to do His Father's will. Our salvation was brought about only by two unions of wills: that of the Father and the Son and the union of Mary's will with God's.

(3) Because of the Virgin Birth, Mary's body was the source of His body. His DNA is hers, not Joseph's. The Blood of Christ is all from Mary's blood.

(4) Christ is Wisdom Itself; Mary is the Seat of Wisdom. When He was a child, that was literally and physically true because her lap was His throne. All her wisdom was from Him, yet His human wisdom was learned from her human wisdom. She learned from Him, yet He also, in His infancy, learned from her.

(5) Similarly with virtue. Her virtue was dependent on His, yet His was also learned from her. He learned obedience from her (Lk 2:51). He was a child, and children are dependent on their parents. This dependence was not removed by His divinity: He was "like us in all things but sin" (Heb 4:15 KJV).

(6) Her three days of loss when Jesus was twelve paralleled and foreshadowed her three days of loss between His death and His Resurrection. Both image His loss of His Father on the Cross when He cried out the words that we find the most terrifying and the Devil found the most delicious: "My God, my God, why have you forsaken me?" (Mt 27:46). Of course, that was not an objectively real loss, but it was very subjectively real. On the Cross, Christ felt utterly alone, forsaken by His

Father; and when He died, Mary felt utterly alone, forsaken by her Son. Women suffer more than men, and no woman ever suffered more than Mary.

(7) She accompanied her Son on the *via dolorosa* as totally as possible. (This was shown strikingly in the movie *The Passion of the Christ*.) Her passion (suffering) was a co-operation with His Passion and its redemptive power, so that she is truly the first and greatest creaturely "Co-Redemptrix". It was a free act of oblation, not a passive victimhood. It was like Christ's, whose life was actively given, not passively taken (Jn 10:18). Mary is our archetype, for we, too, must cooperate freely and actively in our redemption.

(8) When he died, it was her blood that He shed.

(9) His Resurrection and Ascension were paralleled by her Assumption. There are two empty tombs in this world.

(10) She was at Pentecost, birthing His ecclesial body as she had birthed His physical body, both by her divine spouse, the Holy Spirit. This was her second pregnancy.

(11) Her heavenly glorification (coronation) is wholly one with His. Her whole desire is to answer the prayer "Show unto us the blessed fruit of thy womb, Jesus."

(12) Her continual involvement in the world also parallels Christ's. For the Resurrection is not merely an event in the dead past; the Christian confesses, not that "Christ rose", but that "Christ IS risen." He "does stuff to us" in the sacraments and in prayer, and she is with Him always, still actively cooperating in His work.

Her Faith

The world's religions are very different, so much so that it is nearly impossible to give a univocal definition of the term that equally covers, e.g., Buddhism and Christianity. But one feature common to all religions is the need for faith, the need to transcend and add to what sensation, feeling, and reason can deliver to us. Faith is the first necessary beginning of any religion, including Mary's.

The "head" aspect of faith is belief, but the "heart" aspect of it (whether we take "heart" to mean the will or the emotions) is trust, the entrusting of yourself and your life to God. In its volitional dimension, faith is the motive or cause for obedience. In its emotional dimension, it is the motive for trust.

Mary fulfills her role as the Second Eve most essentially here, in her faith. Eve disobeyed and distrusted God's word that eating the forbidden fruit would be death. Her trust in the serpent and her distrust of God were the first step in the Fall; they motivated the act. Mary, in contrast, trusted God's word when it came to her through His angel, even though it was as mysterious as God's command to Adam and Eve; and that trust and obedience were the first step in our redemption.

What, according to Mary, is the reason for faith? It is not abstract but concrete: a personal knowing of God, not just a knowing *about* Him (a *kennen*, not just a *wissen*). This grew from a long habit of personal and liturgical prayer and from the practical wisdom of her Jewish tradition, which has always centered, not on abstract ideas, but on God's concrete deeds in history and human lives.

Her Prayer

This tradition is clear in her Magnificat, which knows and praises ("magnifies") the God of history. Praise is a form of love and an expression of love—we do not praise objects of hate or indifference.

Of course, when we "magnify" or "glorify" God, we do not add to His glory, which is already and always perfect and infinite. What do we add to? Two things: the glory in other people's lives and the glory in our own. In fact we *become* His glory. For, as Saint Irenaeus famously says, "the glory of God is man fully alive"—that is, alive with *zoe*, supernatural life, not just *bios*, natural life.

This "magnifying" (Lk 1:46) is our reason for being, our *summum bonum*, and therefore our joy, our "rejoicing" (vs. 47), for everything attains its fullest joy when it fulfills its reason for being.

It is what we will do forever without being bored in Heaven. Even here, in its shadow forms, it is one of the few things in life that never gets boring as long as it is motivated by love. Love conquers boredom forever. Nothing else does.

This praise is the first purpose of prayer. The second is thanksgiving, which naturally follows it. Thus, in her Magnificat, Mary praises God not only for what He is in Himself ("holy is his name"—vs. 49) but also for what He has done for Israel and for her as Israel's "Savior" and hers (vs. 47). God is praised for His power (vs. 51) and thanked for His mercy (vs. 50).

Mary's prayer to Christ at Cana ("they have no wine") exemplifies prayer's third purpose, intercession and petition. Here is where faith is tested most. Even after Christ's apparent "no" (Jn 2:4), she continues to trust Him. Without coercion, without complaint, she simply presents the problem to Him in total trust. And even after His apparent refusal, she continues to trust: she trusts His response *before* it comes, and she says to the waiters (and to us): "Do whatever he tells you" (vs. 5). Faith does not depend on seeing; seeing depends on faith—as Jesus said to Martha when testing her faith before raising Lazarus, "Did I not tell you that if you would believe you would see?" (Jn 11:40) Jesus reverses the formula "seeing is believing."

At Cana, He let her apparently change His plans and His will because He had planned and willed the whole thing. He does the same to us: when we say and mean "Thy will be done", or *fiat*, or "yes", or "I surrender." When we do that, we place ourselves in the place of power, which is His will, not ours. Then our prayer is answered and our will is done precisely because we ask that *His* will be done. Thus, Mary is our model for prayer, especially the prayer of petition.

The fourth purpose of prayer is confession of and reparation for sin. This is missing from her prayer for an obvious reason. Sinless Mary had nothing to confess.

But we do, and since we are commanded to "confess your sins to one another" (Jas 5:16) as well as to God, it is good to confess them to Mary especially. I'll bet Peter was glad he had her to run to after he denied Christ three times, heard the prophesied cock-crow, felt the burning gaze of Christ upon him, and "went out and wept bitterly" (Mt 26:75). That is a picture of ourselves in Purgatory, where there will be a far deeper weeping than any on earth, but also a far greater joy because, unlike Peter then, we will be on the other side of the Resurrection.

Contemplation and Action

Religion has two aspects, the contemplative and the active, silence and speech, accepting what is and changing what is.

This is clear in the story in the Gospels (Lk 10:38–42) of Martha (the activist) and the other Mary (the contemplative). In the time of Saint Thomas Aquinas, there was a controversy about which life was higher, the active or the contemplative; and Aquinas, with his typical wisdom, answered that the highest life was the mixed life, for that was Christ's life. I think it was Fulton Sheen who united the two by saying that "we must do the works of Martha in the spirit of Mary."

The Blessed Mother did that all her life. It is impossible to be a good mother and not be active. It is also impossible to be blessed and not be contemplative. Mary's life was all religious, and it had two parts, one of which was "secular" —e.g., she helped Jesus learn to speak Hebrew and helped her husband be a good carpenter. Her "religion", or relationship with God, was the Benedictine *ora et labora* ("pray and work"). For, on the one hand, prayer too is a work, and, on the other hand, our daily work is one of our most precious prayers when it is done with Mary's attitude instead of Martha's.

Public and Private

Many politicians have a merely public religion, a "face". Many have a merely private religion, because they are ashamed to be seen as religious in public. Mary avoids both avoidings. She is not a politician. Her religion is both public and private. She publicly obeyed both Roman and Jewish Law, paid her taxes, registered for the census, attended synagogue, and celebrated Passover; but she also "pondered". A lot.

She presented her "private" son publicly in the Temple to God. That is why she found Him there when He was lost twelve years later. She knew where to look for Him.

That is the best place for us to find Him, too. He hides behind a round little thing that looks like bread.

Conclusion

When Tennyson wrote his well-known and well-loved little poem "Flower in the Crannied Wall", he may or may not have been thinking of Mary. But we certainly should. What he says about the flower is essentially what this book has said about Mary:

> Flower in the crannied wall,
> I pluck you out of the crannies,
> I hold you here, root and all, in my hand,
> Little flower—but if I could understand
> What you are, root and all, and all in all,
> I should know what God and man is.

> —Alfred Lord Tennyson (1809–1892)

I was planning to write a book entitled "Flower in the Crannied Wall". It would be an introduction to all the great philosophical questions and all the divisions of philosophy by means of the famous little poem by Tennyson. It would show that in order to explain this one little flower, you needed to do methodology, logic, epistemology, metaphysics, cosmology, theology, anthropology, psychology, ethics, politics, religion, aesthetics, education, history—everything.

Then, while writing this book about Mary, I realized that I had already written that book. It was this one. Mary is the

perfect concrete example of this principle: absolutely everything is right here. We have gone through all the divisions
of philosophy and found her at the summit each time.

You probably thought many times while reading this book
that the title was a fake, that this book was not about Mary
but about the whole of Christian philosophy and life. You
were half right: it was indeed about the whole of Christian
philosophy and life, but it was also about Mary. She is the
flower in the crannied wall.

The reason why this book is not as distinctively Marian
as you thought it would be is because it is more distinctively
Marian than you thought it would be. For we have seen in
this book that what is distinctively Marian is precisely everything in the Christian life. In other words, it is distinctively
not distinctive, especially not specialized, particularly universal.

For although in an obvious sense Mary is distinctive and
unique (there is no other Mother of God, no other Second
Eve, and no other Immaculate Conception), yet, in another
sense, she is the exact opposite of that: she is the universal model for all Christians. All the other saints have some
specialty, some peculiarity, some personal proclivity, some
tangent. But Mary is the center. It is her non-uniqueness
that makes her unique, her universality that makes her particular.

Christ gave us a hint that she was to be particularly universal when He said, "Who is my mother . . . ? . . . [W]hoever
does the will of my Father in heaven is my . . . mother"
(Mt 12:47–50).

Even the thing that is most shocking to her and surprising
and distinctive, that she was picked by God to be uniquely
"full of grace", is our destiny, too. And even her divine

motherhood has a universal aspect that applies to all Christians as well as a unique aspect that applies to her alone. For there is a real sense in which what the angel of the Annunciation said to her is said to us, too. The Holy Spirit must come upon us, too, and the power of the Most High must overshadow us, too, if the divine life (*zoe*) of Christ is to be born in our soul, if the thing that is in us is to be, not just human virtue, but the Son of God (Lk 1:35).

Even the Virgin Birth, as prophesied in Isaiah 7:14 and quoted in Matthew 1:23, is about us as well as her, for we, too, must be born miraculously, not just of flesh and blood, but of God. That is simply the only way to get to Heaven. That is what Jesus told Nicodemus in John 3:5–6.

In giving up her natural fertility, Mary attained a far greater and more universal spiritual fertility, so that "all generations will call me blessed" (Lk 1:48). All Christians call her the "Blessed Mother" because Christ gave her to us, with almost his last words (Jn 19:26–27), which are the whole purpose of this book: to "Behold, your mother."